*THE
TWENTIETH CENTURY
MIND*

THE
TWENTIETH CENTURY
MIND

Essays

on

Contemporary

Thought

by
Donald Atwell Zoll

LOUISIANA STATE UNIVERSITY PRESS

E 169.1
Z6

TO MY PROFESSIONAL COLLEAGUES,
PAST AND PRESENT,
TO WHOM I OWE
IMMEASURABLE DEBTS OF GRATITUDE.

PREFACE

ONE OF THE familiar contemporary musical forms is the "protest song." A few are ingenious and even droll; most of these plaintive ballads seem repetitious and more involved with the ego gratification of the composer-performer than with declamations of significant ideas or even emotions. Overall, the themes of this protest literature—songs, ballads, poetry, articles, books, street-corner harangues—are surprisingly (and often dismally) dogmatic. A perusal of the literature leads one to suppose that protest or dissent in the America of the sixties invariably means a demurrer against a very restricted set of values and an endorsement of an equally limited and doctrinaire list of social goals and beliefs.

I wish to argue that the word "protest" implies a far more flexible range of dissent, and that anxieties over the prevailing shape of things can be expressed in a variety of ways and can espouse a divergent nexus of principles and convictions. The essays in this volume attempt to convey that widened conception of protest and, hopefully, to wed the invective of dissent with the restraining discipline of philosophical detachment.

This book was completed prior to my acceptance of an academic post in a Canadian university. The opportunity to come to know better our northern neighbor and its social and intellectual climate is, for me, a most intriguing experience. However, the points of view expressed in the book are reflections on the American society to which I have belonged and, in smaller part, are my reactions to the contemporary European scene.

I wish to acknowledge the permission of the *Midwest Quarterly* for the inclusion of "The Artist as Academician."

"Conscience, Law, and Civil Disobedience," in slightly altered form, was delivered at the annual Midwest Conference of Political Scientists in 1966.

D.A.Z.

Regina, Saskatchewan
September, 1966

CONTENTS

THE
TWENTIETH CENTURY
MIND

I

THE COMING COLLAPSE
OF THE AMERICAN DEMOCRACY

*Neither this essay nor I are engaged in politics. The matter
under discussion here is previous to politics and springs from
its subsoil. My work is the obscure, subterranean task of a
miner. The job of the so called intellectual is in a certain
sense opposed to that of the politician, the former aiming,
often in vain, to clarify things a little whereas the politician
usually adds to the confusion. . . .*

*Total politicalism, the absorption of everything and of the
entire man by politics, is one and the same phenomenon as
the revolt of the masses. The mass in revolt has lost all capac-
ity for knowledge or devotion. It can contain nothing but
politics, a raving, frenetic, exorbitant politics that claims to
replace all knowledge, religion, wisdom—everything, in
short, really qualified to occupy the center of the human
mind. Politics drains men of solitude and intimacy, and
preaching politicalism is therefore one of the techniques of
socialization.*

—José Ortega y Gasset [1]

In parallel spirit with Ortega, I am not a politician, and,
Heaven knows, I don't want to extinguish light, convinced
there is precious little that continues to shine. Perhaps I am a
"so-called intellectual"; at least that classification sounds
more familiar. How much clarification I can manage must be
left for the reader to judge. I would be tempted, however, to
add one title unmentioned by Ortega: I seem to be listed
among the rebels. In the curious convolutions of ideology,
it appears that the sturdy band of us who espouse the valid-

1 "Unity and Diversity of Europe," in *History as a System*, trans.
Helene Weyl (Norton: New York, 1961), 70–71.

3

ity of traditional truths and values find ourselves in a state of what we hope is polite rebellion against a reigning orthodoxy. It seems that the daring and heterodox liberals of an earlier generation have become the tired and self-satisfied defenders of the orthodox in this generation. What was once heresy has become dogma, and I am forced unhappily to say that it is a dogma whose embracing severity would startle a Metternich, a Calhoun, or even a Maistre. As the spectrum of tolerable social and political opinion narrows in our Republic, many of us are damned to speak our minds, as it were, far from the seats of decision and influence, more or less condemned out of hand as rebels and heretics, dangerous or otherwise depending upon how esoteric and thereby harmless are our criticisms. To be a rebel is never a desirable state of affairs; the title is not intrinsically honorable. And it is not always a question of the validity of the cause that prompts the rebellion, rather it is a matter, I think, of whether the rebel is moved fundamentally by love or hate. To be a useful rebel one must love. He must love those whose ideals offend him, and he must love the ideals that inexorably demand his revolt against the established intellectual order. This predisposition to love need not, in the same breath, cause the rebel to be ineffectual in the personal combat that he accepts as a lamentable but necessary state. To love with passion and imagination heightens one's abhorrence of the unlovely. The twentieth century has seen too much that is unlovely and witnessed more than its share of unreasoned hatred. I would not for a moment add one wisp to that grim burden.

The title of this essay is a melancholy pronouncement: "The Coming Collapse of the American Democracy." We are familiar with all manner of historical explanations for the demise of vast and lofty civilizations; this has been a fixture of historiography for nearly two centuries. A diagnosis of the decay of those political societies designated as "democratic" is less common. It is rather a morbid game to play since we are all, for better or for worse, members of a democratic political society. This implies, among other things, that we face the same historical perils that beset civilizations in general, while, at the same time, facing threats to the maintenance of continuity and order stemming from the character of democracy itself. Surely, one might argue, "politicalism" (to borrow Ortega's handy word) appears to be a general curse among all contemporary societies from the most militant of the Marxist states to our own blissfully pluralistic society (assuming that we are more than merely pluralistic in theory). It is undeniable. After all, however it may embarrass us, contemporary political democracy and Marxism have some common ancestors. We are very prone, partly out of ethnocentric zeal, to prophesy the downfall of communism and, with equal fervor, to reject Marxist predictions of our own decay and subjugation. Yet while we contend that communism has some "built-in" defects that will inevitably spell its ruin and doom, the assertion that democracy may contain such innate imperfections strikes us with dire misgivings which we choose publicly to ignore, covering our doubts with vigorous and even ill-tempered denials. Yet the possibility that democracy may be a seriously flawed political gem remains to haunt us.

All popular political systems and movements appear to contain a universal penchant for excess. One need not climb an historical Olympus to confirm this view; a glimpse of the plain ought to be sufficient. This tendency toward excess in popular political systems so disturbed Plato and Aristotle that they rejected popular government outright and relished in its stead various forms of aristocratic authority. But the democracy of our century is not the democracy of post-Periclean Athens, needless to say, and while Platonic and Aristotelian anxieties may have some foundation, they are not a viable judgment by themselves. Of course, modern democracy reveals the potential of excess and has been frequently guilty of it, but, at the same time, modern democracy has provided a political order in which notable examples of cultivation and refinement have blossomed. It would not be quite accurate to say that democracy *produced* these adornments, but rather that democracy created a situation in which they were possible and, from time to time, may have even fostered them.

This reflection might permit us to conclude, first, that high levels of civilized living are theoretically possible under a variety of political systems, and that modern democracy has provided that sustaining order in a number of instances, and perhaps overall has succeeded in this more often than it has failed. But the roots of civilization are not political, they are something else about which we shall not argue for the moment. The most one can expect of a political system and the political philosophy which spawns the system is that they provide a reasonably secure and continuous base for the development of human talent and the attainment of human happiness.

But how can we account for those times in which modern democracy appears to support civilized and humane life and those times when it does not? When do we have (to use the terms of the late Ralph Adams Cram) a "High Democracy" and when do we have a "Low Democracy"?

I am going to answer that question in a fashion that may appear cynical and even shocking. Democracy as a political philosophy and as a system succeeds in its civilizing role to the extent that it does not take itself seriously. The paradoxical and sometimes fatal malaise of democracy is that its abstract propositions when examined in abstraction are both untenable and self-destructive. Democracy as a formal philosophic commitment is a dangerous fallacy; democracy as an informal orientation, a loose but puissant attitude, *may* be conducive to a way of life desirable in its civility and creative thrust.

But is this not a hideous bit of sophistry? Am I seriously entertaining the notion that when democracy is at its best no one is really believing it? Or, is a democratic state best governed when its rulers have consciously rejected its principles? My answer is that it is necessary for *some* people to "believe" (using the word in its frankly polemical sense), but at the same time it is very necessary that intelligent statesmen never be trapped by the confines of doctrinaire ideology. Let me amplify this observation.

Democracy, if conceived of as being made up of a formal set of propositions regarding human equality, majority rule, natural rights, and so on, has, with certain reasonable restraints, the desirable feature of providing impetus to popular unities, identifications, loyalties, and enthusiasms so long as these abstractions do not become rigid bits of quasi-religious dogma. In the same spirit, democracy conceived of as liberality of mind is a laudable belief for statesmen to hold and an equally commendable quality for politicians to possess.

Democracy is occasionally high farce. And this is not to be viewed with too great alarm since farces are staged and provide a certain catharsis, but farces are not grand tragedies, and a steady diet of farce is hard on the stomach and indicates a certain paucity of imagination on the part of those who are in the business of staging plays. Perhaps one can go along with the flippant Mr. Mencken who found democratic farce wildly amusing and edifying. "I enjoy democracy immensely," he wrote. "It is incomparably idiotic, and hence incomparably amusing. Does it exalt dunderheads, cowards, trimmers, frauds, cads? Then the pain of seeing them go up is balanced and obliterated by the joy of seeing them come down." I confess I cannot manage so lighthearted a view, although the irony is obviously appealing. The concentrated farce of contemporary democracy belies a tragic motif—the signs of a growingly evident decay. But what is the spirit of farce if not the amusement that is derived from the sight of people taking with deadly seriousness that which cannot or does not merit such. These people become the objects of ridicule—effrontery, pomposity, delusions of grandeur are happily shattered or, put another way, the humor of farce is the disastrous consequences which wait upon people who talk about things and act in situations about which they have almost totally no understanding. In the theatre it is laughable; in political leadership it is tragic folly.

But if the finest hours of modern democracy are those in which the broad ideological propositions are not taken seriously, are we to conclude that democracies are governed best by hypocrites and conspirators, callously proclaiming the religion of democracy while proceeding to operate on some other set of ideals? The answer appears to be that this is frequently the case. But the situation is not as grave as might be supposed. In the first place, if no political philosophy or system can be an end in itself, but rather a vehicle toward more elevated values, it would be dangerous indeed if politicians predicated their actions on the basis of what benefited the system, or advanced the dialectic, or proved the most exact replica in action of some abstract political postulate. Is this not one of the features we dislike about Marxism? It follows from this, then, that the normative standard to be applied to political leadership is not how close it adheres to doctrinaire democracy, but to what extent it adheres to those more substantial values we assume that democracy chooses to preserve and foster. One of the pernicious aspects of "politicalism" is the deification of systems.

Moreover, there is a rather respectable body of evidence to support the idea that, even in popular democracies, political authority is expressed through oligarchies. What kind of an oligarchy does one have? Which type would one prefer? A political oligarchy that evidences great public enthusiasm for the slogans of democracy does not by that alone merit favorable judgment. Indeed, the history of democracies suggests that democracy is especially prone, by virtue of its enthronement of the masses, to respond to demagogic ma-

nipulation and, I would go further, that the real slayers of
the commonweal have wielded the destructive sword while
issuing forth ringing phrases about the "dignity of man."

Have we irretrievably indicted democracy? No, but we
have said this much: The "Good Life" is not produced directly by political systems. Democracy as a formal body of
propositions is open to very serious attack. Democracy is
prone to both excess and to decay through the ritualization
of its principles. Democracy must provide for itself a leadership not shackled by its popular dogmas.

High democracy exalts man; low democracy exalts myths
about man. Totalitarianism treads a narrow path on the edge
of the abyss; democracy treads an equally narrow path on
the edge of the gutter.

But not a word has been mentioned about *American* democracy, *the* American democracy. And I have already alluded to its possible collapse. I have admitted (with some
trepidation, I am candid enough to add) that civilization has
and can exist and attain high levels under the political system known broadly as democracy. Now I will take this pulse
of ours. I will attempt to apply some variety of judgmental
criteria to the health of the American political and social
system. I must frankly announce at this point that I am
inclined to view the ends of the criteria as exemplified by the
democracy of Athens and the Roman republic at one extreme (to which I would be prone to add the American
republic before the coming of the Jacksonians) and the
Jacobin Terror at the other.

To establish some guidelines in our investigation, let us
look at our democracy in terms of four categories: *leadership, liberality, ethics,* and *humanism.* These are more than
methodological classifications, these are the primary areas of
democratic corruption. Like specific points of wear in a tele-
vision set, they are the first to go before the whole either
blows up or sputters into silence.

Of the four categories, the problem of leadership may be

the most dramatic and also the most vividly evident. Leadership in a democracy is a matter far more subtle and complex than it is in a forthright despotism or a firmly established aristocracy. Leadership is indispensable to any political system, yet democracy's proclaimed insistence on popular sovereignty means that democratic leadership cannot be built upon an enduring, simple base such as an identifiable class or set of rationally discernible credentials. Yet an elite must be somehow produced. Democracy's historic response has been the *natural aristocracy,* masking the fact with egalitarian platitudes and constantly readjusting the description of those qualities which constitute the necessary prerequisites for entrance into the elite. Democratic political order is expressed, then, in terms of authority by the creation of temporary natural aristocracies (or oligarchies) usually of short duration and with highly varied philosophic underpinnings. Viewed in normative terms, these natural aristocracies have been enlightened or oppressive, wise or desperately incompetent at one time or another. Some have been clearly wicked.

They have not rested on some sole, unitary concept of merit such as breeding, wealth, education, ability, virtue, militancy, and so on, but have displayed these qualities, or some combination of them, with various ratios of significance and at different times. The elites have also differed quite radically in motive. But these differences and varieties aside, historical judgment prompts us to agree, even if we do so grudgingly, that democracy in its higher forms has enjoyed leadership consisting of natural aristocracies largely built around superior wisdom or virtue and, perhaps, possessing sufficient economic substance to permit the cultivation of the first-mentioned qualities. Put it another way: if one concedes that wisdom and virtue are commendable characteristics of an entire society, then that society's leadership should reflect the highest level of those social and civilized attainments. Thus, leadership in a democracy reflects both what sorts of values the society cherishes and, at the same time, the general state of those values in the society entire. If in a democracy, political and social leadership appears notably deficient in wisdom and virtue, then it is because the society as a whole does not esteem wisdom and virtue, or that the general state of these qualities is primitive or repressed. Virtuous government can never rest on mass sentiment; the vanities, stupidities, appetites of the mass man suffocate it, quickly corrupt it. But in a democracy, while the mass does not and cannot rule, it can set limits of toleration in regard to the character of its leadership. When mass sentiment is aroused and unchecked, the result has invariably been the demise or retreat of virtuous natural aristocracies in favor of those bent on private gain by pandering to the grosser whims of the mass. The aristocracies of virtue and wisdom pass and those of opportunistic adventurers follow. The transition is usually slow and in some respects difficult to perceive, since the newer oligarchs appear sturdily moralistic, defiantly humanitarian, invariably replete with benign and homely, or inane sympathies for the downtrodden. And there is usually a Robespierre waiting in the wings; happily, more often than not, he misses his cue.

Further, the transitions of the reigning oligarchies do not occur only in the lofty halls of government, but in many lesser seats of influence, and in many more local organs of institutional authority—businesses, universities, churches, unions, and cultural organizations. It has often been said that under these conditions excellence gives way to mediocrity and this is true in a sense, but many of the New Oligarchs are capable and intelligent. What really happens is that virtue gives way to cunning as the primary political and social asset. There are those of us who cling stubbornly to the identification of wisdom with virtue, believing that they rest upon values objective to men's private opinions and preferences, hence, they are grounds for asserting the superior worth of things and even people. The retreat from virtue as the basis for political leadership arises from the debilitating doctrine that everything is of equal value; just as long as I value a thing, it has an irrefutable claim to value. This dreary sentiment permits the New Oligarchs to claim that their defects, certainly evident to men of reason, are, in fact, glorious attributes; their declaration that stupidity, crassness, cunning, boorishness, and rapacity are social values is highly comforting to those legions of persons for whom any cogent sense of responsibility and self-discipline has long since been obliterated by massive wooings of their vulnerable egos, and by the ridiculous announcement that all men are equal and all desires equally valid.

But in their triumph, the New Oligarchs are strangely uneasy; they are oversensitive to criticism; they begin to imagine all manner of bugaboos, some of them real, some of them fanciful. Being ex-mass men themselves, they know full well the awesome power of the beast they have been feeding and entertaining. They lose sleep and testily begin to lean, lightly then heavily, on dogmatism, conformity, and, finally, coercion. Curiously, they seem to introspect their own defects, ignorances, and intellectual vulnerabilities, since they respond to this reflection by employing greater severity, more self-protective policies, more cunning to take the place of wisdom and liberal virtue.

You know who these New Oligarchs are. They put Socrates to death, they cried for the blood of the Nazarene, they burned witches and made regicide a sport, they soaked the cobblestones of Paris incarnadine.

But these are past crimes and bloodlettings not even identifiable with the American heritage and happily it is largely true. We are not yet sunk into jacobinism, but we are killing each other in the streets, and the "affluent society" has become a slippery euphemism for a national orgy of compulsive greed, vulgarity, and frenetic entertainment. Political leaders have become pseudopaternalistic ringmasters in the ever-accelerating circus of consumption and diversion.

Dare we judge the health of our democracy by its leaders? Cast a critical eye, an unrelenting scrutiny, over the national scene. Do we see the same things? Is this an accurate catalogue? The tawdry figure of Lyndon Baines Johnson as chief representative of this majestic and honorable nation . . . vaudevillians in the U.S. Senate . . . slow-witted ideologues in the United Nations . . . courthouse barristers on the Supreme Bench . . . well-washed, Brooks Brothers-draped brigands at the control of industrial combines . . . gangsters ensconced in trade unions . . . fabulously expensive whores idolized as the ultimate in feminine attainment . . . schoolmasters proudly semiliterate . . . disciples of Hippocrates more at home with the *Wall Street Journal* than at a bedside.

I am prepared to say that we face a critical decline in the quality of the ruling elite, a dangerous deterioration giving rise to most honest anxieties regarding how long significant minority dissent will survive, to say nothing of the integrity of internal government operation. How have we come to this sorry, ghastly, even macabre decadence? It began and continues as a result of the spread of two insidious presumptions: (1) The concept of equality has been extended far beyond the assertion of the sanctity of the person, to an egalitarian leveling which embraces values, persons, opinions, moral acts, and even art. This destruction of a criterion of worth drags us toward a gutter culture in which the lower and less attractive aspects of man's nature become normative. (2) Recognition of differences in social functions has been abandoned. The result is a revel of vanity and the emergence of a peculiar form of snobbery resulting from the implicit demeaning of social functions previously thought of as being of honorable estate. Not all men are destined to play the piano like Horowitz, and it ought not to be a personal tragedy if one cannot. Gone is the pride of function; mass man chooses to be his own ruler, teacher, priest, and admirer. Reckless mobility and artificial status breed cunning and artifice, goad hopeless ambition, and defame honest toil and humble service.

The *dénoument* is farce, just as sure as we hilariously witness Sir Andrew Aguecheek's mawkish attempts to be a dashing lover. But men out of their natural functions are not actors for an hour, but are human beings wounded and dislocated by being victims of their own lack of insight and the manipulations of the callous and the greedy. All humane leadership is at base paternal and benevolent; this man shares with his fellow animals.

And where, you ask, were the virtuous and wise? Where were the "intellectuals," if you will? One replies with a question: What can we do for a society that exalts its scoundrels, trimmers and cads, its exploiters and panderers, to the downgrading of its philosophers, poets, artists, and divines? Whose fault is it that we keep our national consciences under lock and key?

We have evidently chosen the demagogues, the merchandized political image and the emotive rhetoric in preference to wisdom, integrity, and the clash of stark issues. Have we really chosen or have we merely abrogated our opportunity to choose? The fate of the American democracy may hang upon that answer.

The term "liberality" seems to have a connection with the word "liberal" and indeed it does. "Liberal" is a good word, if I can use that simple evaluation; it has had a long and revered history. Regrettably, however, its meaning has become so confused and contradictory in usage that I must avoid it and select "liberality." By liberality, I wish to imply largeness of mind, flexibility of response, dialectical freedom, and regard for logical argument and demonstration. I would even accept "open-mindedness" as a loose synonym provided that open-mindedness" does not imply avoidance of discrimination or some variety of uncritical eclecticism. High democracy always exhibits an atmosphere of liberality, of tolerance for variety and eccentricity, and a happy forebearance of "crackpotism." Democracy has no exclusive claim on liberality, by the way, and such undemocratic social arrangements as feudalism displayed some aspects of it. Certainly liberality must rest upon social order and tranquility, as Aristotle pointed out long ago. Liberality cannot flourish in political licentiousness.

On the fever chart of the decline of democratic societies, one of the most pertinent indexes is the gradual disappearance of the mood of liberality and its replacement by secular orthodoxies, a sort of *subrosa* social totalitarianism—repressive, uniform, and monolithic. Among the first signs to be noted are the belief in social reform by legislative fiat, "programs," popularization of governmental initiative and remedy, pleas for social cooperation, collective altruism, and something called "national unity" or "national purpose." These are usually followed by great faith in the uplifting and remedial powers of economic change and an intensified concern for material wants.

The final stage is the development of a full-blown, publicly articulated social dogma; it is expressed as a public faith which must be unquestioned in terms of ends, although techniques or means are generally acceptable areas of criticism. The dogma invariably is highly moralistic and humanitarian in tone, and it is thought to be sinful for one not to believe it, although it is less sinful for one not to implement it.

This process reveals the slow death of liberality, first, by assuming that human happiness is a matter of social arrangement; second, that man's essential or even primary wants are material; third, that substantial skepticism regarding the prevailing dogma is heretical and sinful.

I need not dwell at length on the American experience in this connection, but permit me to make three brief observations.

First, we are already at the stage of experiencing the unveiling of the monolithic social dogma. We have been told unequivocally what our social "ends" are to be. The blue-print of the "Great Society" is before us in all its absurd yet nightmarish shape. We are busily closing the limits of toler-able political and social debate. We are instructed that it is immoral to entertain certain social ideas, and we proceed to purge from the ranks of the respectable those who are fool-hardy enough to publicly voice their dissent. Humor, wit, satire begin to expire before the onslaught of this social gospel, this new leviathan. The national debate, in conse-quence, grows arid, monotonous, and subservient to expe-diency.

Second, we have developed the "cult of the personality." Tossing aside soul and intellect, we have enshrined the psyche in their place and formed a cultic adoration for its supposed splendors and potentialities. Social psychologists are no longer descriptive empiricists but high priests of the new order, complete with a litany of praise for the precious, if illusive, nature of human personality. All must be sac-rificed or adjusted to the imperious requirements of this suddenly discovered human faculty whose wants are some-how imperative and its constitution so fragile that even gov-ernment must be invoked to protect it from abuse.

Third, we are provided with the ultimate in illiberal machination, the *summum bonum* of the social planner: the extension of the eastern urban tenement across the entire face of the continent with the accompanying élan of the slum settlement house as the bright matrix of community life. It is as if we had given to Harry Golden a sacred mandate to remake America in the image of his wildly over-sentimentalized boyhood. We are, in any case, feverishly in the business of proletarianizing the national life on the con-fused assumption that the true democratic virtues reside in the repulsive maelstrom of the urban lower-class mentality. Our mass tastes blatantly announce this conviction, and it is a heresy to decry it or to point out that the enduring monuments of a civilization are not the productions of the *profanum vulgus,* but arise from individual cultivation and travail in an atmosphere of creative freedom. To make honest endeavor to remedy the plight of the unfortunate and underprivileged is humane and necessary, but this does not imply that one incorporates their values into a social dogma in order to placate their feelings, or to protect their psyches from feelings of inferiority, or to solicit their undeniably awe-inspiring political favor.

America seems to me frightened, unhappy, insecure and, worse, unable to sense her cultural identity. She seems to think liberality is something she cannot afford. She must realize it is an essential she cannot do without.

The state of the national ethics has been much discussed and the decline of morals, if that is what it is, given voluminous public attention. One must be cautious in giving undue emphasis to much that is trivial, however. Nearly every age has been viewed by some as the apotheosis of moral decadence. One must be careful to draw a line between the flux of custom and superficial social habit and the substantive decline of ethical values. The fact that the bikini is *au rigueur* at the beach in contrast to Victorian modesty is not a harbinger of moral collapse any more than the Frug is more decadent than the Tango, or the Sarabande, for that matter. It is a question of aesthetic taste not morals. In some respects, our contemporary democracy has much to recommend it in grounds of common moral behavior. We have appeared to shun public hangings, children's sweatshops, bearbaiting, and the persecution of the insane. I am not much disturbed by the moral implications of our changing tastes, although I may personally find some features of mass tastes repelling, the behavior coarse, or the evolving patterns of life aesthetically rather ungratifying. But I cannot condemn the ethics of the social order on those grounds. Indeed, as far as I am concerned, the more contemporary culture frees itself from the dreary bondage of puritanism the better. Roundheads, jacobins, communists, and social zealots all tend to be rigorous puritans.

However, beyond the vagaries of taste, there are ethical considerations indicative of the quality of social life. This is an immense subject and I can only comment on it with a series of fleeting references. Crime, I think, is a valid indicator to the extent that it illustrates both threats to order and a proper homage to the law. Not all happy societies have to be legalistic ones, but democracy is legalistic to its core and cannot function or survive without the maintenance of legal confidence. Law in a popular democracy bars the door against the barbarian and the diminution of regard for law invites mobism. It is not only a question of a mounting crime rate, but also of the spread of the idea that subjective moral sentiment is a higher mandate than law and that legitimate redress cannot be gained by juristic appeal. Both the rising incidence of crime, which is a potential threat to minimal order, and the popularity of extralegal political action bode ill for the survival of the American democracy.

Next, manners are more of an ethical manifestation than the rude and boorish would choose to admit. The character of public courtesy invariably reflects social self-consciousness and the vitality of humane ideas about living. The decline of manners, even formal courtesy, indicates a lessening of the restraints of self-discipline and the waning of the effectiveness of vital institutions of social control, such as the family, the school, and the church, which are engaged in the business of moral instruction through the inculcation of discipline and habit.

Americans generally tend to view manners with some suspicion, being prone to consider such refinements as effete, foreign, and, in some quarters, even mildly subversive. Also they often preserve the curious notion that manners are, in fact, undemocratic, perhaps borrowing this idea from Thorstein Veblen who dismissed good manners as merely indications of the availability of nonproductive leisure. The frontier and its mentality, virtually unlimited geographic mobility also contributed to America's tendency to lapse into a proud bumptiousness with regard to the civility of deportment.

But it may well be that our democracy is beset by more than an agrarian disdain for Old World courtesy and that our current brand of manners reflects a profound coarsening of our ethical sensitivities and judgment.

I have been saving the most significant for last: this is the widespread abrogation of individual moral responsibility. There is a pernicious doctrine abroad today which states that we are not morally responsible for our acts—"something" is responsible, but not ourselves. This something is usually identified as some deprivation in our environment or some wound to our hypersensitive psyches. There are no wicked people, the argument alleges, only the misunderstood and the underprivileged. This is a palpable absurdity on historical or empirical grounds, but, perhaps even worse, this argument is a foul insult to those multitudes of persons who have found themselves in unspeakable environments, have suffered grievous emotional hurt, and yet have managed to live moral, sometimes triumphantly ethical, lives. In the darkest slums of our megalopolises, as well as in the ghettos and abcesses of ancient cities, there have existed gallant souls whose ethical characters rival those of saints. How are we to explain these people? Are we to tell them that their struggles were superfluous and without necessity or meaning? That they are freaks, indeed? Clearly, if we toss away the idea of wickedness, we must also jettison the concept of individual goodness, and we shall then drown in the slough of environmental determinism. The final outcome is not the freedom that democracy boasts, but a particularly obnoxious form of slavery, bondage to undifferentiated appetite and the uniform hell of pre-engineered and allegedly sanitized environments.

The facile rationalization of all desires and the abolishment of the concept of legitimate individual guilt is, in my view, the most serious manifestation of ethical decline. The crumbling of the civic ethic has been instrumental in the collapse of a host of political systems, democracies included.

The antithesis of *humanism*—in the sense that I now elect to employ the word—is the conception that the human being is less than human, is a "thing," a mechanical contrivance, a "statistic," a miniscule cog in a gigantic social engine, a unit of energy as against a unique spiritual entity. Kant wisely demanded that human beings always be treated as "ends," never as "means."

All large and complex social organizations run the risk of dehumanization. Size alone is a threat to the proper status of the individual. Edmund Burke, anticipating the emergence of the "mass state" nearly two centuries ago, counseled that a man should know and love his own "little platoon," his immediate social involvements, that only by doing so could larger loyalties be developed without risk to individual identifications. We are all painfully familiar in our century with the debauch of humanism in totalitarian movements, and we condemn these as easily as we do their ideological nature and ends which we are prepared to denounce as immoral. It is simple, as it were, to accede to the moral lessons suggested by *The Animal Farm* or *1984*, perhaps even *The Brave New World;* it is less obvious to grasp the essentially dehumanistic tendencies of mass movements which invoke creeds to which we would tend to give assent and support. If the goals are designated to be "freedom," "equality," "justice," "progress," "civil rights," and "prosperity," we tend to minimize the risks to the preservation of human identity. The fact is, however, that democracies can often become quite as dehumanistic as avowedly totalitarian systems; the difference is not only one of degree and, perhaps, of insignificant degree, but also of cultural style. One of the reasons why many Americans do not fear domestic dictatorship is that they assume dictatorship would take some exotic form similar to those they have observed in Germany, Japan, or Russia, and they cannot imagine such conditions as an indigenous set of arrangements and customs. An American dictatorship would be no more like Nazi Germany in style than it would resemble the Zulu empire of Chaka—it would be dictatorship American plan, complete with George Washington, Valley Forge, the Stars and Stripes, the "home of the brave," the World Series, Captain Kangaroo, and Mother's insipid apple pie. It would appear to be the apotheosis of democracy—and, of course, in a sense it would be. When political faith becomes confused with religious faith, one is advised to keep his luggage packed.

It must be remembered, too, that a person does not go to bed one night a human being and arise the next morning as an animated social organism in terms of society's viewpoint. The transition from a humanistically oriented society to a dehumanized one is by slow degrees and is difficult to detect. It involves subtle shifts of attitude, and it appears in habits and patterns of thought which do not in themselves appear very important or far-reaching.

Let me suggest a couple of illustrations drawn from collegiate life that are by themselves quite trivial, but are also provocative indications of the growing acceptance of dehumanistic attitudes.

Not long ago I attended a meeting of the faculty senate of the institution where I am currently employed and during the discussions of that body a dean, a ranking administrator, frequently referred to the "servicing" of students—"how many students can we *service* under such and such a program" and "what percentage of students could be *serviced* in classes of a certain size" and so on. The verb caused me some anxiety; the thought of servicing the undergraduates was startling, to say the least. On a deeper level, the remarks and their meaning were something of a revelation. I wondered how well students would like being "serviced." This is only a mild beginning. Contemporary man can expect to be more and more "automated" in the interests of would-be social efficiency, his life an IBM card in some gargantuan social "memory bank."

Another example. Not far from where I now sit a women's dormitory complex is being completed, and it will include a large dining facility. Do you know what this facility is being called? It is designated, I pray temporarily, as a "food service center." Can you imagine a place where human beings break bread together (itself an immemorial ritual) being entitled a "food service center"? Are educational institutions to become educational filling stations? One is haunted by the vision that the student of the future will sleep at night in a "somnambulant recovery facility," have breakfast in the "food service center," and attend classes for "educational servicing." And if he is of a religious turn of mind, during the day he can drop into the "spiritual reorientation clinic."

Trivial, you say, and just an example of democracy's admitted vulgar passion for sententious euphemism? Perhaps, but these are tiny slices. Multiply these isolated illustrations several thousandfold and you can graphically calculate the drift toward the demolition of humanism.

If you would prefer a broader-scoped example, consider for a moment that one of the marks of a humanistically conditioned society is a sensitive regard for individual privacy. Our benevolent founding fathers gave great emphasis to the protection of the individual from "unreasonable searches and seizures," a concept of right hard gained by our English ancestors. Ponder for a minute the present state of privacy in our republic. I realize that it is difficult to generalize, and conditions vary locally, but I would contend that it is chilling to speculate to what extent our lives are and can be monitored by a growingly omnicompetent state. I gather we even are increasingly spying on ourselves, "bugging," if you will, each other for commercial advantage or sheer lascivious curiosity. It could well be that our modest castles will become electronic studios; they are already denuded of most of the nominal defenses of privacy. We are apparently of the opinion that walls, hedges, courtyards, separate rooms, and drawn shades are immoral or antisocial.

The increasing dehumanization of American democracy results in large measure from the sacrifice of individual prerogatives and traditional formulations of the necessities of human nature to the metallic strictures of popular ideology. One must admit that technologically developed, urban, interdependent cultures must adjust some of the grand isolation of essentially agrarian life patterns. However, the critical shift is from the concept that the end-product of societal organization is individual human happiness to a conviction that human beings are individuals only in pleasant but archaic theory, and that they are, in reality, collectivisable means to some abstracted social purpose. This is the point of departure that heralds the democratic demise—in the long run human nature cannot be denied.

Do we, then, face the collapse of the American democracy? Have we so abused leadership, liberality, ethics, and humanism that we are at the point of either self-destruction or the inability to survive in an obviously hostile world? Indeed, we may be better able by dint of sheer power to persevere in our external combat with the barbarian than we are able to cope with the barbarians in our midst. After all, when the last draft card has been burned, the last peevish placard thrown down on the public thoroughfare, and the last idiot has immolated himself with the aid of a can of gasoline, there will remain a considerable phalanx of the honorable and steadfast. But this phalanx is more easily taken from the rear, its lingering potency strangled by decadence and faithlessness.

We are now terribly vulnerable, and this century may well see our strickened and abject defeat. This capitulation, if it comes, will not as likely be the result of some ghastly passage of missiles as it will be from the creeping incursions of barbarism on a land once proud, virtuous, and, in the best sense, pious. Democracy is a dangerous political equilibrium; benevolent aristocracy is probably a safer course, but it, too, is not immune from corruption. In any case, danger can be a stimulant to accomplishment. We may be moving at an accelerating speed to our national death, but I do not think it is an inevitable course, as history itself is not an inevitable dialectic. Our salvation rests in cultural humility and introspection; our desperate foe is the excess of popular vanity. But throughout the ages, vanity has been an awful opponent of virtue. Standing alone, it is an unequal struggle; where virtue conquers, it does so through an alliance with love.

We cannot pretend to love all men. I cannot see how democracy can dare to do so. But we can try to love what men have been and what men can be, the realized human essence, and I do not think that democracy can survive without trying to do so.

That we are on Matthew Arnold's "darkling plain," I have no doubt, or chained in Plato's "Cave," if you prefer the classical allusion to the romantic one. We have reason to shun and fear the darkness of the captivity of the human spirit, and such a state of blackness is not brought about by flicking some gigantic and ominous switch, but by turning out the lights—one by one.

II

THE FAILURE
OF AMERICAN CONSERVATISM

As GOLDWATER'S PRESIDENTIAL aspirations died in the *sturm und drang* of the voters' will, we can confidently assume that the Grand Old Party sat down to council, to conduct the traditional postmortem, albeit this one morosely contemplating the most disastrous political rout of the century. Goldwater, the political leader, was dead. Aside from the conventional commiserations, Republican reactions were undoubtedly mixed, ranging from unalloyed joy on the part of the roughly treated "liberals"; covert satisfaction from those who had supported him in the interests of the party image but who were delighted to recover lost personal influence; to genuine perplexity among party tacticians, many of whom had serious convictions regarding the potential political strength of the Arizona Senator's ideological posture. Perhaps, too, the defeated candidate's intimate coterie mused over the hemlock cup, bereft either at the thought of ideological rejection from the body politic, the precious dogma spurned, or the loss of the very newly gained control of the party machinery. In any case, these members of the Goldwater entourage should have reflected on their participation in the most ill-conceived, horrendously botched presidential campaign in the history of these curious folk dramas.

Who or what had died? This was the paramount question confronting Republican retrospection. Was the fault to be found in philosophic untenability or inadequacy of political execution? To over-simplify: Had the Republican party chosen something called "conservatism," and had this alternative political orientation been overwhelmingly rejected by the electorate, or had there been something singularly and decisively wanting either in the candidate himself or in the

25

supportive techniques employed to gain him the decision? Should the party make a major change in ideological direction, or attempt to analyze and correct deficiencies in organizational practices and campaigning skills?

It is quite obvious what the response to these assorted questions was. With much pious breast-beating, the GOP elite began to disassociate itself from the repudiated conservatism and the formidable body of party eclectics, many of whom were more or less safely ensconced in the halls of Congress. It turned to a hastily conceived "golden mean," spoke of "fresh approaches," and extended the olive branch to the party liberals still more or less sulking in their tents. It castigated "extremists" and other schismatics, laying the blame for the party's disaster at the door of exotic ideologists and antimainstreamers. While the Goldwater forces were not totally disbanded in the face of this burst of organizational self-righteousness, they retreated to local areas of favorable sentiment and launched "educational" associations and other proselytic ventures hoping, it would seem, to identify themselves with intellectual and literary conservatism, a feat they had not previously managed to effect.

What was evident in all this agonized reappraisal was that the party leadership conceived the broad alternatives as two in number: one was "conservatism," identifying this as being the credo of the Goldwaterites and the other was "liberalism," as associated with the eastern wing of the party and the "progressive" élan of the Eisenhower honeymoon. Was this a very difficult choice, they mused? What reasonable man could not draw the inevitable conclusion? Conservatism had been crucially defeated because it was not a viable political creed, but rather a cultish aberration, undeniably attractive in some aspects, but aside from its nostalgic appeals, lacking in both popular support and relevancy to national issues. On the other hand, the liberal persuasion showed signs of life. What GOP rejoicing could be evidenced was surely the result of the candid support of this point of view; Mr. Lindsay had become mayor of New York City, even with the double handicap of running against a Democrat and a "cultist" (Mr. Buckley), and Governor Romney continued to exercise formidable control of a state whose political composition would seem to favor the Democrats. Hope, if any could be found, must reside in embracing the liberal cause.

But was there any plausibility in hope? Perhaps, as far as the Republicans were concerned, this was the fundamental conundrum. The GOP might well become a perpetual minority party, increasingly weak and ineffectual. All manner of dissecting the political variables gave credence to this grim opinion; there were the matters of age dispersion, urban centralization, Negro enfranchisement, and so on. If the liberal path was inevitably to be followed, no comfort was to be wrought from the fact that the Democratic foe was already in possession of a militantly liberal image and always able to up the ante in that sort of an auction—how to "out-liberal" the traditionally "liberal" national party?

So the GOP ponders its fate. Its deliberations in this connection are doubtless interesting in and by themselves, but Republican introspection in another sense touches very directly on the future role to be played by political conservatism in American life. It would appear that the Republican party has concluded that American conservatism is a failure. Such a decision cannot help but affect the vitality of conservatism, however the GOP may misconstrue the character of indigenous conservative political thought. In declaring conservatism a failure, the Republicans may be operating on a number of quite dubious hypotheses. Among them may be these: (1) Senator Goldwater was a conservative. (2) Senator Goldwater was always wrong. (3) Senator Goldwater was overwhelmingly rejected at the polls because he espoused conservatism. (4) The Republican defeat represented the rejection of conscious conservatism and conservatism (of any variety) has no substantial political appeal. (5) The nature of future decisive political issues will remain fundamentally the same as of those that have traditionally structured American political combat.

It might be hastily added that there is some reason to suppose that political analysts in the Democratic camp may share with their GOP counterparts a belief in the reliability of these conclusions. It might be remembered by party strategists (although one assumes they rarely lose sight of it) that one of the oldest and most prudent maxims of the craft of politics is to never judge situations in terms of one's wishes or prejudices, but only on the basis of uncompromising realism. One detects, even so, in Democratic glee over the 1964 decimation of their opponent the somewhat miasmic opinion that their victory settled for once and all renascent conservatism. If Democratic strategy is to be conceived on this axiom, it may well be that Democrats may be in for a rueful surprise or two. Conservatism remains latent even within the ranks of that party, and it is certainly a contemporary political myth that conservatives are all invariably Republicans, or that the only conservatives in the Democratic fold are Southerners opposed to racial integration. Such notions are interesting because they reveal the widespread misconceptions regarding the nature of conservatism. It might be argued, for example, that one of the pet whipping-boys of the Republicans on foreign policy questions, Senator Fulbright, is in fact far closer in his views to conservatism in the historical sense than those who are his critics and who are often identified by the press as being conservatives.

What we are not seeking here is the salvation of the Republican party, politically or spiritually; it will have to carry on as best it can. Neither is it our intent to offer tactical advice to the Democrats. Our aim is to assay the true political condition of American conservatism, and a convenient means of doing so is to make an analysis of the discrepencies in GOP reasoning.

The first fallacy was the assumption that Goldwater was a conservative. This was essentially a failure in historical awareness and philosophic fastidiousness, prompted in large measure by Goldwater's persistent invocation of the term on his own behalf. No one can legitimately quarrel with a subjective definition of a term, provided the user is clear and consistent. However his insistent employment of the word "conservatism" had the regrettable result of effecting wide public exposure to a definition that was historically and philsophically confusing and that tended to make conservatism synonomous with nineteenth century individualism and a revival of frontier virtues and attitudes. That Barry Goldwater was not a conservative is a virtually uncontestable observation; he does not even fall under Clinton Rossiter's spacious and somewhat incongruous definition.[1]

In the past decade there has been a torrent of *belles lettres* purporting to explain to everyone just what conservatism means. It has been a pet passion of the so-called conservatives themselves and, although there is considerable bickering about the details, it is fair to suggest that it is possible to get a functional definition of what can be called "historical" or "self-conscious" (Rossiter's phrase) conservatism. One cannot here examine this complex problem of definition, but on the most rudimentary scale, Goldwater fails to emerge as a "historical conservative," albeit he appeared in agreement with some aspects of it.

If he did not in fact campaign as a "conservative," what political genre is his? This is not an easy question to answer, partly because the gentleman from Arizona did not produce what could be described as a cogent political philosophy. For this he cannot be justifiably castigated, it should be added, since the number of presidential candidates who presented such a coherent body of theory are rare indeed. At

[1] Clinton Rossiter, *Conservatism in America* (Knopf: New York, 1956).

the same time, it is equally true that he obviously sought
after the mantle of a political philosopher. If Goldwater
could be classified in some categorial scheme of political
theory, he appeared most directly a product of nineteenth
century liberalism, at home with William Graham Sumner
and the *laissez-faire* economists.

Goldwater's political inclinations were distinctly
bourgeois. At base, his primary interests were economic, not
philosophical. He was a nationalist, almost an "old school"
jingoist. His attitudes toward the state and its prime agent,
government, revealed a Spencerian hostility. He was manifestly a social darwinist, a calvinist (small *c*) in ethics and
the embodiment of frontier pragmatism, his Episcopalian
connections notwithstanding. His views on international relations were astonishingly radical, using the latter term in its
more precise sense; he was a simplistic moralist and a "devil
theorist" in world politics. He would have given a truly
conservative statesman like Metternich an acute case of
nerves.

Such formulative ideas and instincts as Goldwater revealed them were scarcely in the deeper conservative tradition. In orientation historical conservatism has been aristocratic, not *bourgeois;* it has hardly supported *laissez-faire*
economics. Conservatism has been cosmopolitan, being suspicious of militant nationalism. It has been concerned with
the issue of governmental legitimacy and arbitrary usurpa-
tion, but it has held the state in some reverence and has
acknowledged the necessity of state power. Conservatism
has been resolutely antisocial, darwinistic and broadly catho-
lic (again, small *c*) in its ethical stance. Flexibility, realism,
and an abhorrence of moralistic ideology has invariably
marked conservative attitudes in foreign affairs.

Beyond these considerations, it is possible to reasonably
discuss politicians in terms of their temperaments, their
styles, their behavioral peculiarities and connect these, in

turn, to more extensive ideological orientations. By this test, too, Barry Goldwater did not appear to be a conservative politician. Given this criterion, Adlai Stevenson, John F. Kennedy, or even Franklin Roosevelt appear to be more typical of the breed of Burke, Disraeli, and Churchill than does Goldwater and, indeed, a case could be made and has been made that one or all three of these Democratic personalities were more distinctly conservative than such publicly labeled Republican "conservatives" as Herbert Hoover, Robert Taft, or Goldwater. The latter's penchant for conceiving of his political efforts as "crusades" (taken, perhaps, from Dwight Eisenhower's linguistic arsenal), his dour political evangelism, his avoidance of wit, gracefulness, self-criticism, and color in favor of earnestness, dedication, and unvarnished candour suggest temperamental dispositions generally not identified with traditional conservative statecraft.

Despite some denials on the point, Goldwater in action and emphasis consistently departed from the cardinal conservative belief—that politics is not the primary activity of man. Ortega y Gasset's repulsion over "politicalism" or Quinten Hogg's good-natured, if flip, definition of the conservative's affirmation as "fun and foxhunting first" are very akin to the indignation of Edmund Burke with "sophisters, economists and calculators." And all of these sentiments are foreign to Goldwater's deadly serious adherence to political remedy and his peculiarly ambivalent feelings about the proper scope of state power.

If his announced philosophies and public image revealed little kinship with conservatism, his choice of staff and advisors and, indeed, his more vociferous volunteer adherents, appeared alien in both character and opinion to the historical flow of American conservatism. If it was true that the Goldwater forces, inside and outside of the party corpus, consisted in large part of "extremists," of self-appointed anticommunist vigilantes, defenders of Caucasian or Nordic supremacy, pathologically ethnocentric nationalists, or Spencerian social primitives, then the Goldwater "wing" hardly, in the wildest gyrations of the imagination, could purport to espouse conservatism. The question of just who were Goldwater's core following is yet to be fully explained. A preliminary deduction might be that his pre-convention support was generated by four principal groups: (1) a loyal and dedicated cadre of persons essentially attracted to the man, and persons whose identifications were primarily regional and cultural rather than in terms of somewhat more esoteric ideology; (2) substantial numbers of people motivated to support Goldwater out of the hope that he would support, directly or indirectly, what was their single-cause conviction, *e.g.,* anticommunism, race segregation, economic special interests. These "one-shot" interest groups, to whom he did not overtly make an appeal, nonetheless felt that he might be secretly sympathetic to their assorted causes. Included among this group were doubtless substantial elements of the so-called "radical right"; (3) a number of the conservative intelligentsia whose frustrations regarding the vitality of "practical" conservative politics caused them, somewhat frenetically, to endorse him, overlooking his unfamiliar aspects to cling to his few conservative tendencies. (4) A sizeable group of the GOP center who frankly yearned for the halcyon days of Eisenhower's hypercautious moderation (what Peter Viereck has called "the last Indian summer of hucksterdom"). As Goldwater consciously bore toward the ideological center while his party prominence increased, they concluded that their interests were more in harmony with his than with those of Rockefeller, Scranton, or Romney and that Goldwater might be a more virile campaigner.

With the possible exception of group three, *none* of these Goldwater backers were conservatives. But who were the twenty-nine million who voted for Barry Goldwater for President of the United States and why did they do so? And what does the answer to that question have to do with the unfolding role of conservatism?

It may be possible to frame a coherent answer to these questions by inquiring further into the state of Republican cerebration. If the GOP is now wrong in thinking that Goldwater was a conservative, it is equally in error if it thinks that his campaign proposals and criticisms were totally without merit. While it will be reasonably simple to demonstrate, a bit further on, that the Goldwater-Miller campaign was almost inexplicably ill-conceived and mismanaged, GOP strategists would blunder if they were to assume that Barry Goldwater did not occasionally make good sense, and that great masses of the electorate did not realize he was making sense, even if they did not on an overall view decide to vote for him. The slogan "In your heart you know he's right." is now an ironic jest, and its undeniably pompous rhetorical quality made it the brunt of levity during the campaign itself. Its effect was blunted, too, by his frequently intemperate and ill-considered *obiter dicta*. However maligned, this phrase carries even now a stubborn element of truth. The truth it conveys is not about issues, but about attitudes and what it proclaims is the fact that not all political issues dare be resolved on the basis of self- or collective interest, painless nostrums, or appeals to popular vanities. It contains a subterranean plea for political realism and the avoidance of mass egocentrism. He did an inept job of communicating this message, yet the adumbrated entreaty of the slogan was heard.

To ascertain when Goldwater was "right" would entail a long catalogue of specific issues and would be at best a largely subjective evaluation. It is tenable, though, to hazard the generalization that he was both inclined to be right and politically effective to the degree that he was truly conservative. He struck four main conservative chords in his race for the presidency. They were his most telling petitions, and there is evidence to suppose they received favorable attention even from a huge contingent that did not mark his name on the ballot.

Intermittently, he raised the issue of the future status of the individual, the scope and station of the individual man in the emerging political system and his relationship with government and society as potential threats to his sense of identity and purpose. As a candidate he neither delineated a cogent philosophy of responsible individualism nor discussed at any length or depth the predicament of self-cognizance and its protection in an increasingly rabbit warren-like culture; he did announce the issue as being a significant and ominous one. This declaration touched a raw nerve in the contemporary American, and this concern for individual prerogative and the defense of human variety is an ancient conservative tenet.

Second, he attempted to draw attention to the social perils to be found in theories of man and society which are rooted in economic reductionism. Man must be something more than an ambulatory stomach, and the health of the polity cannot rest exclusively on state-stimulated affluence or a concept of human welfare solely preoccupied with economic ameliorization. While Goldwater essentially was a man of business, who viewed the troubles of the republic in economic terms, he did voice the opinion that solutions to national problems must transcend some rejuvenated doctrine of "two chickens in every pot." The fact was that there were already two chickens in most pots, and the problem of sheer economic survival was uncommon among the great percentage of the voters. While "pocketbook" issues were still highly influential in political attitudes, they had lost some of their intensity and had been partly replaced by concerns primarily sociological or even psychological. Indeed, one of the mounting ironies in American social metamorphosis was that the attainment of certain levels of material affluence did not provide the expected gratifications; and frustrations attendant upon this realization began to be felt in the shifting character of political preoccupations. Goldwater did not obviously understand this fully or comprehensively, but perhaps he had more of a glimmering of its emergence than did Lyndon Johnson, whose political strategies were quite orthodox and possibly even obsolete, however successfully he rebuilt the conventional Democratic coalitions in the face of the vapid GOP alternatives.

Third, he raised the issue of order. Once more, much of what he had to say about order was either confused or imprudent, but it has been a long time since a major political figure in this country has talked frankly about it, although the public has been aware of the spiraling threat to civic order reflected in the galloping increase of crime and the phenomenon of massive civil disobedience and the diminishing respect for legal authority. Since Plato the problem of order and its maintenance has been central in political philosophy and has been almost invariably linked to the broader area of morals. Except for some rather dismal moralistic homilies, Senator Goldwater did not vividly invoke the moral issue; of course, to do so would have been to revolt against the established mores of political practice, habits forged in the brazier of pragmatism. But whatever else may have been his shortcomings, he knew well one simple proposition: the fundamental responsibility of government is the maintenance of order and the protection of its citizens. This dual obligation has become immensely complex in the twentieth century and the techniques involved are of necessity subtle and variegated; and there is some justice in the anti-Goldwater jibe that his basic solution was merely to corral the wagons. But it should be pointed out that he annunciated the desirability of action and castigated the reckless refusal to acknowledge the existence of threats to public order. The obtuse fact is that it is dangerous for law-abiding men to walk the public streets of major cities after dark, and

all the pseudosociological rationalizations and windy senti-
mentality currently being disseminated cannot obscure this
fact. We have seen the Watts riot—long after the election
had passed. To assume that the American public does not
know or does not care about burgeoning disorder is errone-
ous and politically naive. Conservatives, right or wrong,
have historically taken the problem of order very seriously
indeed and have frequently been willing to jeopardize their
popularity by so doing.

Finally, Goldwater perceived the fact that there are limitations to the sphere of governmental action, not only regarding the legitimacy of such action, but as to what it is
possible to remedy by state intervention. While his notions
about the legitimacy of governmental activity and his conceptions of the "private" and "public" domains were both
often inconsistent and scarcely conservative, he was graphically aware that certain major social issues could not be
resolved by increasing governmental regulation and supervi-
sion. He was enough of a Burkean to grasp the idea that not
only are some problems matters of altering the hearts of
men, but also that inappropriate governmental interference
in these situations has the pernicious result of stiffening
hostilities, stimulating tensions, and generally encouraging
the superficial avoidance of the more radical factors in the
problem. Governmental fiat is not a universal panacea and
one supposes that nearly everybody must know this, but it is
frequently forgotten in the cheap meliorism of American
politics. He reminded the electorate of this conservative, but
also truly liberal, conviction.

If Goldwater was not a conservative in a comprehensive
sense and, at the same time, was most effective in appealing
to the latent political sensitivities of the public when he
occasionally espoused conservative ideas, it would be very
strange to conclude that the GOP defeat in 1964 was a
rejection of conservatism. It is probable, however, that the

Republican party may be currently entertaining this dubious deduction. One suspects that while the Democrats—at least the Democrats of the liberal camp—publicly voice the same belief, a hard core of professional party tacticians know that it is not so and within the majority party are perhaps as many sympathetic to conservatism as are in the GOP organization.

Three main factors account for his public rebuff. They are not mysterious by any means, but glaringly apparent. At least two of these factors have been given copious attention by political analysts. The first of these involves the conduct of his campaign, an undertaking that must be characterized as a textbook illustration of how not to carry on a presidential race. Even before he had secured the nomination, the Arizona senator had begun to alienate the swing vote by exhibiting a marked regional and social parochialism. His choice of William Miller was a piece of catastrophic political judgment that even at the time seemed wholly incredible. What Goldwater did not need was a confraternal barracuda. His political acumen did not improve as the campaign swung into gear. He lacked an overall strategic plan and appeared to avoid almost studiously the hard Eastern urban encounters that were pivotal, a fact known to any sophomore political science major. He proceeded to develop a personal image that was a somewhat more rugged facsimile of the fearless frontier marshal, unsophisticated and guileless but true of heart. It was the image which had stood Eisenhower in good stead. But the performance was already out of date: Eisenhower himself as a folk hero was diminishing in stature as the "frontier revival" receded and the Kennedy era shuffled the emphasis away, perhaps permanently, from bucolic practicality and rusticated virtue.

Goldwater punctuated this display of simplistic virility by confusing candor with proportion, and he blundered into naive and even ill-tempered exhibitions of impromptu diagnosis and cure. His remarks on foreign policy were often flatly astonishing and must have been a source of sharp embarrassment to some of his advisors in this field, a number of whom, incidentally, were men of undeniable competence, regardless of whether one would choose at all times to agree with them. It seemed rather clear that he listened but little to staff advice, because an examination of his "braintrust" reveals the presence of a number of people who are sophisticated political and international analysts whose advice could not have been that bad. That the Senator basically distrusted intellectuals and, perhaps, even policy specialists, was well known throughout his political career. Even in his leisure moments he seemed to prefer radio hams, mechanics, and New West businessmen to members of the intelligentsia. In this, his tastes were not very much different from those of his opponent and, indeed, they are men of a somewhat similar breed—two men with big hats who are at home at barbecues and who wrinkle their eyes in the sunshine. But to Johnson this was a secondary adjunct, even a dispensable personal factor to be repressed or partially abandoned as the situation dictated. Not so with Goldwater; his plainsman egotism was more direct than Johnson's, if less intense overall, because it was less fired by ambition. Obviously Goldwater's partiality for personal amusement damaged his campaign; he could not separate the palpable fun of being a candidate with the discipline required for victory. Win or lose, he was going to be himself and this may have been admirable in a way, but the trouble was that it was a luxury no candidate can successfully afford and Goldwater as Goldwater revealed a man starkly inadequate to the demands of the American presidency. It may well be that Lyndon Johnson was similarly inadequate, but the deficiencies were less cavalierly flaunted to an electorate whose powers of precise or thoughtful discrimination cannot be said to be very potent.

A quixotic candidate, a bumptiously conceived image, an improvised and careless campaign battle plan, a lethargic and obsolete organizational structure, and even a lack of a sense of elemental political timing were handicaps critical in themselves, but these were made unbearable by the bifurcation of the party and the sullen withdrawal of the anti-Goldwater Republicans. Internecine hatreds and the not-altogether unrealistic surmise that Johnson could not be beaten caused many a party chief to take to his tent to contemplate the state of the world and to dream of fresh conquests in 1968 or 1972 or 1976. It is one of the truisms of American politics that to lose an election is an unpleasant happening, but to lose control of the party organization is a calamity to be avoided at all costs. Some spurned GOP satraps clearly saw that the most expeditious means of recovering lost party leadership and patronage was to allow the eager Mr. Goldwater to immolate himself on the spears of the Johnson host. The reasoning was sound, if cynical.

The second major factor in the GOP debacle was the demonstrable and perhaps insurmountable advantages enjoyed by the Democrats. Curiously enough, however, the noisy Mr. Humphrey notwithstanding, these advantages were not so much ideological as substantial and particular. The *nominal* Democratic strength was in theory decisive and the Kennedy assassination increased that abundance of Democratic potential. Lyndon Johnson, even as incumbent, was not a charismatic figure; the Democratic strength rested on a coalition not on an all-embracing ideological conviction; and Johnson offered no novel or even compelling justification for his continued leadership, but he made few overt political errors and this was all he needed to do. The point to be made is that any GOP victory was to be built upon making sizeable inroads among nominally Democratic voters, voters nominally Democratic as a result of factors not deeply philosophic. If Eisenhower's pair of triumphs mean anything, they must suggest this. But in 1964 the GOP was incapable of mounting such an attack, either in terms of personnel or the power and scope of their reasoning. To win, Johnson essentially needed only to avoid flagrant disasters and pose as a reasonable, experienced, eclectic chief executive. The Republican problem was far graver, of course. It involved a successful political revolution which party members lacked the power and skill to pull off, but which also would have been premature and abortive in any case.

The third explanation is less obvious, but perhaps equally decisive. It was the fact that the GOP saw dimly, if at all, that success meant a major reorientation of basic political issues. The Democratic coalition stood, a compact welded together by loose interests, but interest groups drawn along the lines of conventional political issues and separations—labor *v.* management, government welfare *v.* private initiative, easy money *v.* hard money, ethnic consciousness, old class differences, and so on. But the provocative question was: Did these "classic" issues and separations reflect the latent political interests and anxieties of the electorate? If they did not, then the Democratic coalition stood on something less than a rock-bottom foundation and the dramatic and perceptive redefinition of fundamental social issues might cause it to tumble. If the Republicans ignored this possibility or were unable to effect such a redefinition, then there was no reason to suppose that the Democratic entente would expire. In short, with no viable alternative other than the traditional Republican rebuttals, even when slightly shifted by Goldwater, the electorate would again turn to the omnibus Democratic party. This was exactly what transpired in 1964. The failure was partially the fault of the GOP itself, it was partially the fault of Mr. Goldwater, but it was also partially the result of the timing of the evolution of social ideology. The time was not yet ripe, as it were, in 1964.

If the hidden base of American political consciousness was changing, is changing, what is the general nature of this change? It is a tangled, obscure metamorphosis and it is largely inarticulated by the citizenry, but its principal outlines are observable. In greater part, it is a shift from economically rooted concerns to primarily social ones. Economic issues are no longer provoking the intensities of feeling and class identifications that they have done in the past. We face a politics of affluence, even if we are short of the goal of full employment and still have pockets of nagging poverty. Indeed, the hue and cry of 1964 was not for bread and jobs but rather an appeal for particularized economic ameliorization arising from the recognition of virtually universal national prosperity—"We are all so well off, isn't it shocking that we still have people under-fed and ill-housed?" But on other fronts, the traditional economically oriented political issues have lost their sting, too. Labor, in the main, is less militant and increasingly concerned with working out broad social reform rather than wrenching simple economic concessions from employers. The business community, despite mumblings and grumblings, is basically content, adapting with surprising ease to the patterns of a semiwelfarized state. Class consciousness along economic lines of demarcation is rapidly being blurred as any analysis of rampant suburbia will attest. The rise of material well-being and its attendant problems of consumption and amusement have made issues of leisure-time employment, educational purpose, and status increasingly more significant than archaic oratory about the full dinner pail.

As economic anxieties retreat, social ones advance. The city, the megalopolis, urban problems, crime, race, leisure, psychological alienation, public mental hygiene, even public morality, and a hundred lesser social problems and issues begin to prey more voraciously on the American political mind. Much is written about these matters and, occasionally, politicians vaguely allude to them, but, by and large, the American politician is steeped in a traditional school and he is slow to adapt. The result is that political debate is largely ungermane to the real perplexities that gnaw, sometimes even unconsciously, on the American public. Having no alternative, the voter makes his choice between the conventional alternatives, but because the issues which structure these alternatives grow less significant and are of less moment to him, he increasingly makes his choice on the basis of some nebulous attraction to the personal attributes of the candidate. One of the obvious results of this split between public political issues and real political concerns is that the voter will very likely select on the basis of the individual characteristics of the candidates rather than the solutions to problems they represent and advocate. Because in the silence of the candidates on matters that touch him, the voter can only hope his chosen candidate will act with intelligence and effectiveness in dealing with these unspoken challenges. The failure accurately to identify issues leads to the rapid decline of party responsibility, the deterioration of the vitality of the government's legislative branch and the disturbing rise in executive power and presidential authority. The "cult of personality" in politics leads to uncritical paternalism.

Central to the social anxieties of our time, which are fast becoming the antecedents of political opinion, is the question of individual man in a speedily altered environment in which many political precepts seem lacking in relevancy. Eventually to be sacrificed is the long reign of political moderation, constructed principally on a nineteenth century foundation, and a correspondent groping toward more extreme political alternatives at both ends of the ideological spectrum. This tendency toward more extreme experimentation is hardly conservative in nature, and this fact is significant in the sense that it illustrates the shift of emphasis springs not from ideological persuasion but from a frantic search for some meaningful ideological posture. The hunger is for new prescriptions in a mood of philosophic fluidity. Since the emerging climate of American politics is highly unsettled, it is not initially favorable to any political orientation, but because the existing party lines are drawn on traditional issues, the mood cannot find adequate expression within this system. The end-product must be an inevitable realignment and rebalancing of political forces to reflect the transmutation of issues. The labels may remain the same, but the internal composition of the political parties must eventually undergo rather thorough revamping. The best guess would be that this realignment would produce, on the one hand, a party reminiscent in general type of the Social Democratic parties of Western Europe, countered by a "conservative" opposition built much more comprehensively on social theory and less upon the vestiges of nineteenth century liberalism. Political realignment will mean the increase of self-conscious and responsible conservatism.

Two other factors indicate not the demise but the resurgence of thoughtful conservatism, beyond the matter of the adaptation of party power to shifting issues. One is the obsolescence of *twentieth century* "liberalism," particularly in terms of imaginative appeal to the young, a group with an almost innate distrust of orthodoxy; and liberalism has become a contemporary orthodoxy with the same lethargy and smugness characteristic of orthodoxies everywhere. The adventuresome and inventive spirit of liberalism in the days of the New Deal has been replaced by administrative parochialism and the "young turks" have grown old, contented and dogmatic. The youthful rebellion can take a number of directions and perhaps the most prominant one is "antipoliticalism" and a sort of transparty partisan nihilism. But it is also true that reflective and intellectually rooted conservatism is an attractive "heresy," too, particularly if it remains realistic in its orientations and thereby provides an alternative to the disillusionment of the young with timeworn shibboleths purveyed by liberal democrats. Much "mileage" is gained by conservatives in their appeals to the college-aged by the fact that they are an articulate and spurned minority. This is a valid observation *if* the conservative message is the historic one rather than a sordid *melange* of bigotry, reaction, social darwinism, and pompous nationalism. That the conservatism of Peter Viereck, William Faulkner, Reinhold

Niebuhr, Peter Drucker, or Willmoore Kendall has not touched the youthful sensitivities would be a major oversight. And, too, the conservative does understand the anxiety about a society of "ticky-tacky" houses and *bourgeois* suffocation and has some remedies to suggest.

Second, conservatism may yet play an important role in American politics for the somewhat circuitous reason that as yet no attractive conservative politicians have emerged on the national scene and the impact of such a man or men might have most provocative effects. Further, there is reason to believe that such personalities, even candidates, may be forthcoming for reasons already suggested, as well as for the fact that the popularity of serious conservatism, even in academic circles, is a fairly recent phenomenon. Not only is it true that popular movements lag behind theoretic speculation, but also the contemporary crop of politicians still springs from an educational milieu largely if not exclusively dominated by the expiring gasps of pragmatism and the social criticism of a then-adolescent social science. Self-designated "conservative" politicians have almost to a man revealed a taste for oversimplification of issues and remedies and a covert hostility for intellectualism, whereas more traditional conservatism has recognized variety and complexity as concommittants of political discussion and has been suspicious of hypernationalism and social *a priorism* rather than exhibiting an animosity toward intellectual excellence or even preoccupation. Yet even these crude distortions of the conservative world-view whetted appetites, even as such political ideas and images have repulsed many, including some intelligent conservatives. Even Goldwater and his rejection may have paved the way for the emergence of truly effective, charismatic conservative personalities.

What would such a personality be like? Perhaps the answer is best framed by describing what he would not be like, at least as a point of departure. He would be a twentieth century man, not a nineteenth century one. He would not be a dour evangelist or an apostle of the "gospel of work" or of some visionary "American dream." He would not be a purveyor of "old wine in new bottles," but new wine blended from ancient formulae. He would not be an economic reductionist or, indeed, a paladin of the NAM any more than he would be an apologist for trade unionism or ethnic minority interests. He would not be a proposer of programs and masterplans of social engineering with a tangential catalogue of platitudinous political and social virtues and vices, but he would be an advocate of prudence, circumspection, and equilibrium. He would not be a moral relativist, but a politician convinced that humane and successful government must rest on ethical verities.

He would certainly be a humanist, in the older sense of that word, displaying an unusual blend of realism about human proclivities and the need for order with a compassion springing from a sense of the importance and significance of the individual man, his dignity, and his proper sphere of action. The conservative politician would startle some by his candor, his unorthodox stripping away of banality, but this would be relieved by his profound sense of style, stressing dignity, cultivation, wit, and even graceful eccentricity. He would not be a "man of the people" or even a merchandized image of popular wish-fulfillments, but a distinct and well-defined personality, neither bland nor obtuse. He would make it clear that when the electorate selected him they would not be buying a "pig in a poke" since he was the consistent projection of his stated ideas and, also, that he was not trading on any collection of quick-acting social nostrums, that he was "selling" ideas and principles, not legislative miracles or painless and nondislocating reforms. He would talk about philosophic concepts and most certainly about "ends."

These are manifestly broad and generalized descriptions, one might argue, hardly a field guide for the recognition of conservative politicians or a chart of the anatomy of conservatism. This is true, but it is also as far as one can legitimately go in prophesying the characteristics of future conservatively oriented political spokesmen. The reason for this should be obvious: conservatism is not an ideology, but a state of mind; it is an attitude, historically shaped and ethically conditioned, toward the reception and contemplation of political and social issues. It has never sponsored a manifesto nor announced a slate of objectives and, for that matter, it has neither projected a blanket indictment of change nor has it supposed that change of itself denotes improvement. Rather it has operated from what it considered rationally conceived propositions regarding the nature of man, morals, and society, and to say that conservatism is dead is to say that a bulk of the formative and persevering ideas of Western civilization has perished. To say in another context that "agrarianism" is dead, in the same fashion, would be to say that men no longer relish the smell of moist earth or the vernal drama of greening fields and forests. No one can *abolish* tradition, one can only choose to disregard it. In the last analysis, that is conservatism's greatest asset: at root, it shares in men's most essential desires and affections. When conservatism prospers it remembers this, when it is in retreat it has forgotten it.

But even if one may conclude that conservatism, as we have broadly conceived it, is to be with us always in one shape or another, that deduction does not answer the question of whether American conservatism has failed in the immediacy of political struggle. To some, the answer may be a ready "yes"; they are satisfied with the drubbing administered to Barry Goldwater in 1964 as conclusive evidence. Others may say "no," but use as their defense a paraphrase of George Bernard Shaw's remark about Christianity—conservatism has not failed because it has never been fairly presented.

The first conclusion is untenable and the second descriptively inadequate. It is true that conservatism has not been fairly presented, at least in the hustings, but all the news from the political wars is not that bad. Conservatism is livelier than some mere holy and esoteric truth carefully preserved but publicly unloved and unwanted. This brand of political gnosticism can lead conservative intellectuals into the spinning of dialectical webs as their principal occupation. The vital and real sense of conservative mission lies elsewhere—in the bosom of the American electorate.

III

CONSCIENCE, LAW, AND CIVIL DISOBEDIENCE

IT WOULD BE superfluous to dwell upon the fact that Negro protest groups and others opposing prevailing policies and practices have revivified the issue of civil disobedience. Highly organized and ideologically sophisticated minority organizations have seen fit to use a variety of devices to exert pressure to obtain redress, including demonstrations, boycotts, "sit-ins," "kneel-ins," "teach-ins," "wade-ins," "freedom rides," draft card burnings, and even self-immolations. These techniques have been described as "nonviolent civil disobedience." The term "disobedience" is clearly intended to mean refusal to obey existing patterns of both social practice and law (to include federal, state and municipal statutes). At least in theory such "disobediences" could be mustered against all judicial restraint against prerogatives deemed "rights" guaranteed on the basis of appeals to such diverse sources as the federal constitution, theories of "natural rights," and even the Holy Scriptures. The act of conscious, premeditated disobedience to law is defended on the ground that such actions are justified by "conscience." This is to say the individual possesses the broad mandate to judge the moral efficacy of specific laws by an appeal to his private conscience, and subjective moral conviction enjoys a primacy over statutory law. This position has been undeniably assumed by leaders of the civil rights movement, the claim expressly made by Dr. Martin Luther King.

It is not a novel claim in the history of American political and social ideas, but it is quite obviously a question of immense import; inferences drawn from the initial proposition are far-reaching, touching not only the fabric and character of the society, but as well our fundamental, even foundational, legal precepts and institutions. However, the question of the tenability of the argument cannot be discussed solely in social terms or justified by some claim of historical expediency. The assertion of the primacy of "conscience" over law invokes issues essentially philosophic. The question demands an examination of the nature of conscience and the implications such an analysis necessarily provides. An appeal to the sovereignty of conscience brings with it the same philosophic responsibilities that result from a similar claim for the imperative nature of such phenomena as intuition, revelation, or the transmigration of souls. There is a vivid, if regrettable, history of individuals who bore public witness to being motivated by the truth of private conscience and were nonetheless subsequently judged by responsible observers as being guilty of appalling anti-social acts, murder, pillage, and rapine. The blunt fact of the existence of the psychopath and his frequent invocation of inner direction and justification cannot be overlooked.

But the assertion that maniacs have often claimed the supremacy of private conscience is clearly not an argument against either the real existence of conscience or its corresponding moral injunction anymore than similar acts of insanity committed by disturbed persons under the mad presumption that they were "instruments of God" are valid evidence against the existence of a supreme being. In fact, there has been in our national intellectual discourse a respectable defense of both the existence and supremacy of private conscience. Such an argument was explicitly made early in the national experience by Roger Williams in 1644 in *The Bloudy Tenent of Persecution for Cause of Conscience*.

It is worth a passing note that Williams' subsequent theological antagonist, John Cotton (*The Bloudy Tenent Washed and Made White in the Bloud of the Lambe*, 1647), took on the question of conscience not by denying its existence, but rather by insisting on a normative evaluation of it, arguing that if conscience is thought of as being some variety of internal guide, some transcendentally inspired directive, the matter of "good" and "bad" conscience must be faced. The existence of the conscience must be dealt with as a matter of "true" conscience as opposed to "false" conscience, one being a valid divine manifestation, the other of demonic character. But the determination of the authenticity of the counsel of conscience cannot be made by an examination of the conscience itself, but rather by recourse to publicly available scriptural doctrine, in short, by comparing the dictates of conscience to what Cotton presumed to be the laws of God. Cotton has not emerged from his exchanges with Williams as a popular historical disputant, due in large measure to Williams' defense of religious toleration and Cotton's limited Calvinism, but Cotton did resolutely contest the nebulous conception of conscience as an unquestioned justification for acts of private will, a view Williams' rhetoric seems to suggest.

Two hundred years later, Henry David Thoreau was to vigorously reassert the primacy of conscience and, indeed, provide a full-blown rationale for civil disobedience much used by current advocates of this form of social protest. In this oft-quoted passage from Civil Disobedience (1849), Thoreau makes the claim unequivocal:

Can there not be a government in which majorities do not virtually decide right and wrong, but conscience?—in which majorities decide only those questions to which the rule of expediency is applicable? Must the citizen ever for a moment, or in the least degree, resign his conscience to the legislator? Why has every man a conscience, then? I think that we should be men first, and subjects afterward. It is not desirable to cultivate a respect for law, so much as for right. The only obligation which I have a right to assume is to do at anytime what I think right.

In his *Slavery* (1835), William Ellery Channing offers an account of conscience both more rigorous and sophisticated than Thoreau's and one which seeks to avoid the radical subjectivism of the author of Walden. Referring to the individual, Channing comments: "His conscience, in revealing the moral law, does not reveal a law for himself only, but speaks as a Universal Legislator. He has an intuitive conviction, that the obligations of this divine code press on others as truly as on himself."

Neither Williams, nor Thoreau, nor Channing, nor contemporary defenders of the supremacy of conscience have provided what might be described as a systematic exposition of the nature of conscience viewed from the perspectives of metaphysics or ontology. Even Emerson's discussions of this matter, couched as they are in the somewhat graceful language of an urbane pseudoplatonist, fail to do other than to suggest that conscience is a sort of organic receiving set, tuned, fortuitously, to the Over-Soul. Emerson is not notable for his specificity of language, to say nothing of his insights into the wisdom of Plato and Plotinus, but he does imply that perhaps two broad conceptions of conscience are possible for us by sheer dint of his synthesization of one of them.

The first conception identifies conscience in terms of the Judeo-Christian or Neo-Platonic tradition by describing it as a superorganic attribute by which private intuitive wisdom is possessed by man, such wisdom emanating from the Godhead or from some other supernatural quarter, expressing itself in terms of moral guidance or reflection, and inducing a state of remorse or recognition of man's inherently fallible moral nature. This is evidently the connotation that clings to the word in popular speech and its explications range from the subtleties of Neo-Orthodox theologians to the somewhat simpleminded remonstrances of parents to children or the homilies of soap-opera heroines.

A second conception of conscience has emerged from the analysis of human nature provided by Freudian psychology and subsequent psychological thought under Freudian influence. In brief, this conception of conscience identifies it as the "superego," choosing, by and large, to abandon the more conventional word in favor of the psychoanalytic terminology. Fundamentally, the superego-conscience is the socially conditioned segment of the ego that results from the psychic encounter of the individual with the world of experience, paramountly, the experience of the radical relationships of the family. It is a moderating, censoring apparatus, inhibiting, screening, rejecting the streams of unacceptable libidinous demands. It becomes an expression of social and familial indoctrination presumed to provide the personality with required socialization. But beyond this cursory description, there are several propositions relating to the Freudian conscience that expressly concern any philosophic consideration of conscience.

First, conscience or superego is naturalistic and organic. Second, it is not primordial or atavistic, but is essentially hostile to the innate, a priori elements of the psyche. Third, while the "first order" mechanism of the personality possesses a generality of a trans-cultural variety, the conscience is an indigenous social product, the result of individual social involvement. Fourth, the conscience is not so much a moral arbiter, a guide to positive moral action, as it is a censor, a restrainer of instinctual appetites that are socially inappropriate. Fifth, the conscience as a mechanism is not only morally neutral, but can either be a detrimental element to emotional well-being under certain circumstances or a wholesome leaven to the personality.

In making a choice between these two basic views of the nature of conscience, it is obvious, the ethical issue apart, that a root choice must be made between a conscience considered as an immaterial "thing," its origins necessarily to be found in some variety of metaphysical abstraction, or conscience considered as an organic attribute (albeit immaterial as well) of man, classified broadly as a neurological phenomenon. The extremes are apparent—conscience as an epiphenomenal mystery or conscience reduced to psychobiological categories, possibly explainable in cybernetic mechanics, or as "trapped universals" in neurological circuitry.

There exists, however, a methodological distinction. Any claims made for the existence of a transcendental conscience appear to rest on evidence finally reducible to the subjective privacy of the testimonial. These claims, impossible to discount totally, are, equally, impossible to assert categorically. Propositions about the transcendental conscience are manifestly nonfalsifiable. Nor can they be demonstrated empirically or logically. They are very likely, in fact, to be accepted or rejected by individual men on the basis of the recognition or supposed recognition of like experience: "I believe you have had this experience you describe, because I, too, have heard the still small voice in the night."

Conscience conceived of as being a socially induced, naturalistically originated facet of human personality has its problems of proof, too, although somewhat eased by the less grandiose claims made on its behalf. If one has never seen a conscience, it is certainly a fact that no one has ever seen a superego, either. But it is a salient characteristic of contemporary science that the existence of a great collection of cornerstone entities cannot be verified by direct observation or even by traditional empirical demonstration. Their existence, however, can be asserted on the grounds of their indispensability for the maintenance of cogent and viable theory. If this argument might be made to support the existence of the superego, why could it not, then, be employed in the defense of the transcendental conscience?

The reason is quite apparent. The naturalistic conception of conscience is, when all is said and done, mechanistic. It is certainly nonnormative, except in a functional sense. It does not counsel in terms of dogmatic pronouncements; as an organic mechanism, it enjoys a state of fundamental neutrality, especially in ideological terms. It is a conveyor, not an oracle. The same cannot be said of the transcendental, theistically oriented conception of conscience. It prescribes presumably, but when it does, its prescriptions are alarmingly confusing, contradictory, and it displays all manner of peremptory nonconformity. Its prescriptions are finally reducible to individual prescription, if not caprice. From this observation, it must follow that a lack of generality and uniformity deny to the transcendental conscience that logical requiredness enjoyed by conscience as mechanism. It cannot be "necessary" for the maintenance of a general theory while it lacks any evidence of internal consistency.

There remain three alternative positions that might be adopted. One would be to reject as untenable the entire idea of conscience. Beyond this, the choice must be made between the two comprehensive attitudes suggested. It is obvious, returning to the opening remarks of this essay, that those espousing civil disobedience have decided to employ conscience as a justification for the organized resistance to law. The question now becomes: Which of these conceptions of conscience have they in mind? Which of the two do they wish to incorporate as a fundamental precept? And, what are the consequences of this choice?

It would seem likely that those who propound the doctrine of civil disobedience and the supremacy of private conscience over law are divided on this matter, some embracing one conception of conscience, some the other. But I would think it reasonable to assume that the far larger of the two groups would be comprised of those advocating a transcendental view of conscience, since a large proportion of the leadership of civil disobedience groups are clergymen, or those announcing dedication to Christian principles. For this reason, it may be useful to proceed with a discussion of the implications of this point of view, taking what we might call the minority view later.

Those who defend civil disobedience on grounds of conscience, defining this term as a superorganic moral agent, face two formidable difficulties. The first is the weakness of the argument in defense of this conception of conscience itself. This defense must finally embrace irrationalism of some variety, enjoining its own special brand of mysticism. Be that as it may, the second difficulty is no less troublesome and it suggests a stunning paradox.

Civil disobedience endorses, by its very nature, not only a philosophy of the conscience, but also a philosophy of law, indeed, the law it sees fit to abrogate and disregard. Defenders of civil disobedience must and have developed a conception of the essential nature of jurisprudence to their own satisfaction, either as a conscious extension of their basic beliefs or as some inarticulated notion of the nature and purpose of law. The leaders of the civil disobedience movements are clearly not against law, per se, but apparently are opposed to some types of law. Actually the civil rights movement as a whole has used law as an instrument, often with effectiveness. One might say, quite fairly, that the civil rights movement has a pragmatic view of the desirability of law.

Barring some supporters of civil disobedience who are philosophic anarchists at heart and to whom law in general is a sinister conspiracy, the civil rights leadership appears to have these basic attitudes toward law. First, law is manifestly limited in scope; it must be secondary to something else. That "something else" appears to be an adumbrated notion of some higher moral sanction made known through the channels of individual conscience. The apparent supposition is that there exists a common moral order among men, certainly an absolutistic ethical position; but, on the other hand, law is viewed as particular and temporal, limited by a superior moral code. But this is not, assuredly, any assertion of natural law, since natural law is rationally discoverable, publicly evident, superinforms civil law and is discernible not significantly through the channels of subjective consciences. The civil rights leaders are certainly not natural lawyers; if they were, their attack upon what they believe to be the iniquities of prevailing civil law would not be through the means of disobedience, but rather through a rational assault upon the character of existing law, claiming the guidance of an evident natural jurisprudence as a criterion.

Second, law is a man-made contrivance, frequently, so the civil rights leaders contend, an instrument of repression and inequality of treatment. Their convictions about justice when pursued full-round are strikingly similar to Thrasymachus' observations in *The Republic*. To them, law is an instrument, even a weapon, threatening or beneficial not in terms of itself, but in terms of its social effects upon those social interests and values they hold to be of prime significance. At best, law is an instrument, direct and ephemeral, of social amelioration.

Consciously or not, the civil rights-civil disobedience proponents are thus legal positivists. But they are, more accurately, only half legal positivists. It is certain that they would find little sympathy for Austin's definition of law as "the command of the sovereign" with its Benthamite conception of sovereignty as the will of a quantitative majority. Certainly they could not accept law as social utility in its fundamental sense if they wish to preserve either the notion of the supremacy of the individual conscience, the existence of a higher moral mandate, or, indeed, some appeal to "natural rights." Strangely enough, however, the doctrine of civil disobedience on grounds of conscience leads inevitably to such a paradox. Moral absolutism must be abortively wedded to legal positivism; the very metaphysical predispositions that underlie the argument of conscience must be turned upside down to justify the idea of the artificiality of law.

Let me put the paradox another way: it may be said truthfully that those who practice civil disobedience choose to make discriminations among specific laws according to their own conceptions of justice. Thus, they would quite readily be willing to talk about "good" and "bad" laws. Why not, then, "good" and "bad" dictates of conscience? This inference the civil disobedience advocate could not accept, and perhaps, from his standpoint, this is a sagacious reaction. He finds himself in one paradox if he accepts the idea of "good" and "bad" conscience; he would be in the situation of agreeing that only "good" conscience takes precedence over "bad" law, and "bad" conscience must certainly be subordinate to "good" law and so on into a *reductio ad absurdum.* Still, he does deny that conscience is open to the same ethical judgment which he enforces against law. He has put conscience beyond judgment, but he denies to law any other mandate (eschewing law as moral, historical, or philosophic sanction) than the positivistic conception of law as being direct social action guided by an omnipotent majority. This crude dualism is hopelessly paradoxical.

At this point, the civil disobedience supporter may fall back to other defenses, in particular, the hallowed language of "natural rights." But here again he appears to be in deep logical trouble. He may choose to profess adherence to the doctrine of natural rights, inalienable and immutable, beyond the powers of lawmakers to abrogate or abridge, but if he does so his implied conceptions of law and of civil disobedience are irreconcilable. If he presses his positivistic legal philosophy, he runs face into the fact that such philosophy must rest on a denial of natural rights. He is invited to read Bentham's scathing denunciation of natural rights. Quite the contrary, legal positivism proceeds from the assumption of social utilitarianism; "rights" to individuals are those freedoms of action society deems it desirable to extend in its own interests for a limited period of time. Perhaps the civil rights adherent would choose to embrace a contemporary utilitarianism with its corresponding "analytical jurisprudence," but if he does he must abandon his claims of conscience, natural rights and, above all, civil disobedience.

It cannot be assumed, of course, that the proponent of civil disobedience will choose to defend the supremacy of the individual conscience in such transcendental, absolutistic terms. Perhaps perceiving the difficulties such an assertion implies, he will rest his case on a naturalistic conception of conscience, discarding the Christian or Neo-Platonic metaphysic and selecting as a definition some variety of explanation fundamentally in accord with the conscience equals superego viewpoint. Here, at least, he can make a tenable reconciliation, if he chooses, with some philosophy of juridical nominalism. It would be a legitimate marriage. He need not flirt with natural law to be consistent, he can argue civil disobedience in respect to law without even needing to circumvent the majoritarian or consensus theories of law.

While this vision of the conscience has the advantage of consistency with legal positivism or activism, from the standpoint of civil disobedience it does open one other unsettling line of thought. The superego-conscience is unequivocally a product of the socialization of the individual. It represents the encroachment upon the ego of *social* norms, even more the subjective influences of the familial encounter. Whatever else it may be, this conscience is an acquired facet, a unique product of "individuation." Its common or collective content is social, representing some variety of communal consensus. It is at war with the presocial elements of the psyche and even, at times, is in a state of tension with the ego entire. How, then, can a claim be made for its superior mandate over what would seem to be either the most authoritative and enduring of all socially normative expressions or the explicit articulation of the inherent rational order—law?

It would appear that only three alternatives present themselves in response to this question, admitting that this conception of conscience excludes the possibility that conscience represents the manifestation of some higher stratum of intelligence or divinity. First, it might be contended that this conscience is not in fact the result of enculturation at all, but represents the surfacing of rudimentary and essential a priori constituents of human nature or, put another way, conscience as the "primordial self." This might prove promising save for the fact that any claim for the universal character of human nature must be made in terms of the correspondences that exist in lower, nonindividuated levels of the personality, not in the more novel integrations of the superego. Further, from Freudian subjectivism or Jungian *geistewissenschaften,* conscience represents an extreme form of separation from the taproots of man's radical nature.

Second, the primacy of the socially originated conscience might be made in terms of a "general will" theory. This argument would have to presume that conscience was an innate, almost instinctual, facility that enables individual men to respond to the imperious dictates of a "collective conscience," a *volonté generale,* a ubiquitous omnicompetent social mind. So far so good, but two objections must be immediately entered. First, one is trying to repair a naturalistic theory by an appeal to a metaphysical abstraction, hardly a tidy philosophical enterprise, but let that pass. The real obstacle is that any theory of a general will must unhesitatingly endorse some doctrine of the omniscience of the majority. Law is obviously beyond appeal, however law is specifically conceived; Rousseau, for example, limits his definition of law, but so defined it stands unchallengeable. How could one obey and disobey the general will at the same time?

Third and last, this concept of conscience could be justified by a candid and full-blown egocentrism. This argument could state the proposition that individual judgment is the sole and solitary criterion and reduce all forms of social standards to arbitrary and unwarranted invasions of the primacy not of conscience alone, but also the self. This contention has the merit of lucidity, but its inferences lead, often hurriedly, to such exotic notions as contemporary "objectivism" or, more traditionally perhaps, to philosophical anarchy. This latter persuasion has had serious and thoughtful espousal (certainly Thoreau moved close to this conviction), but it seems almost incredible that those who defend civil

disobedience or, indeed, seek to further the interests of Negroes or other minority groups should find much comfort in
the doctrine of anarchy. The pervading fallacy in Thoreau's
recommendations for reform and the attendant techniques
was that these prescriptions were viable only within the very
institutional framework he was tangentially seeking to abolish. Civil disobedience is nonsense anywhere save in a legalistic state. Gandhi's much admired movement in India was
possible and, in a sense, successful because his opponents
were the British. History fails to reveal an illustration of a
successful campaign of nonviolent civil disobedience directed against a political establishment that did not feel
itself inhibited by the cords of law. The advocates of civil
disobedience would doubtless quickly respond that, of
course, the technique was designed to take the above-men-
tioned situation fully into account. No doubt both true and
clever, but it militates against the endorsement of anarchy.

In sum, it is difficult to see how the defense of a naturalistic conscience offers a way out of the paradox that con-
fronts those who make claims for the supremacy of private
conscience over law. But to cast serious doubts on the superior mandate of the conscience does not in itself either prove
the sanctity and infallibility of law or invalidate civil disobedience as a means of obtaining redress. Law, any corpus of
law, is and should be open to attack in some form—and
attack outside its own provinces. Further, it is sharply apparent that law is a manifestation of political doctrine; indeed,
it is hard to imagine its being anything else. It is additionally
reasonable to enter the plea that the question of differentiat-
ing between a "law" and an "order" is still a respectable
dialogue. Whatever terminology one chooses to use, all
edicts that men are asked to obey may not carry the force of
law. Political philosophers since Aquinas have acknowledged the possibility that disobedience may be a legitimate
act. Why not, then, on the basis of private conscience? On
what grounds if not this?

One proposition appears persuasive: disobedience can never be an act of individual will. Explanations of this contention, e.g. Aquinas or Locke, have been sufficiently influential that the proposition has been evidently acknowledged in the broad realm of the relationship between the individual and the state. But it has also been challenged in a number of specific instances. In all these cases, such disobedience has been rooted in the belief of the primacy of the individual over society, a by-product, if you will, of social atomism. The justification of individual disobedience rests on the assumption that the interests of the individual and those of the community are basically hostile and that the former must take precedence. This in the long run must be denied, if not on the ground of social organicism, then by virtue of the vital concept of equilibrium and adjustment between claims of liberty and order. It is simply a fact, not a posture of cynicism, that the multitudinous variety of mankind contains within it those who disobey by acts of will, either upholding the supremacy of self-interest or believing themselves the possessor of some puissant nonpublic truth. The state of social existence requires the denial of these private trangressions, even admitting that among the repressed number may be an infrequent martyr or prophet.

To argue that disobedience as an act of individual will cannot be legitimate is still not to contend that disobedience, per se, cannot be legitimate. What about disobedience as an act of two wills? Or four? Or four thousand? Does this change the case? Surely two murderers are as reprehensible as one, it might be urged. The numerical factor is not of itself critical; disobedience to law justified only by the dictates of private conscience is untenable regardless of how many private consciences are grouped together. At the same time, it is feasible to contend that disobedience could represent a *collective* act. Such an assertion would draw a distinction between a group disobedience as a pooling of individual wills and a sense of collective purpose. Such a distinction has been rather persistently made in the history of political thought from Aquinas to John Stuart Mill. However, disobedience as a collective act can be legitimate only when certain conditions are met. I think the conditions are these: (1) The justification for disobedience must rest not on an appeal from conscience, but from articulate reason, however bizarre that reason may appear to others. (2) The disobedience must represent the pursuit of some common and publicly identified objective shared by the group. (3) The disobedience must be conceived as a political gesture and act, and it must result from the exhaustion of all existing political remedies. (4) Such disobedience should not by intent or accident directly impair the reasonable interests and welfare of other private persons within the community. (5) Those committing the disobedience must be aware and willing to accept the consequences that may follow from their acts. (6) The act of disobedience must involve only those fully cognizant by virtue of age and comprehension of the purpose and nature of the refusal to acknowledge lawful authority.

The current advocates and defenders of civil disobedience have chosen to take their stand on the primacy of conscience. In doing so they have selected the most precarious of justifications. After examining the alternative rationale outlined above, it is undeniable that the contemporary civil rights movement has rejected any such corresponding view, judging both from the statements issued by authoritative spokesmen and in the actual conduct of its disobediences and demonstrations. However more limited its philosophic implications and modest its claims to omniscience, a justification for civil disobedience based upon the pursuit of publicly acknowledged political ends, candidly identified as a group interest, has the substantial merit of being an internally consistent and intelligible point of view, regardless of its intrinsic rightness or wrongness. Moreover, it tests law more directly in that it meets legal mandate squarely on the basis of social consensus rather than on the questionable grounds of individual priority. In short, *if* any case can be made for civil disobedience, it would seem that it must be posited in these terms.

Why, then, do not the leaders and theorists of the civil rights movement choose this sturdier defense? The answer must be that it is sturdier only in the sense that it is more dialectically sophisticated and that it places the ultimate resolution of the conflict in the hands of social judgment. From the standpoint of the protest leadership, the first consideration is essentially frivolous and the second too precarious to be undertaken seriously. The selection of the defense of conscience arises from two quite expedient considerations. First, social consensus, even when moved by the techniques of civil disobedience, is too slow and untrustworthy; and, second, the existence of internal, intraorganizational political factors require a more complex view. The problem for the civil rights leadership is apparently more than devising a persuasive advocacy of their objectives, either in the intellectual marketplace or in the streets; while the leaders orate against the "white power structure" or governmental despotisms, it is clear that they have constructed a power structure of their own. The very momentum of their militancy requires something more than logic. more than political dialogue; what is required is the creation of the myth of omniscience, not only in the persons of the leaders, but in the private identifications of the followers. Thus, the primacy of conscience and the confused, if vociferous, challenge to the rule of law.

The result is to do more than muddy the waters of debate or, in application, to mar the civic tranquility with burdensome incivilities. The more serious implication residing in these ill-considered justifications of civil disobedience is that assault, disturbingly accelerating, on the traditional conceptions of the supremacy of political and legal process over individual or mass caprice. The appeal to conscience in the civil rights movement is but another skirmish in the mounting contemporary attack on political remedy in general and is an illustration, too, of a growing clamor for forms of social action that supersede the deliberative and compromising instrumentalities that have been the distinguishing feature of American and European democracy. The primacy of conscience suggests a new absolutism in the same spirit that the "antipolitics" of European youth, the perverse statecraft of leaders of emerging nations of Africa and Asia, or, indeed, the reckless actionists of our own domestic "radical right" seek to substitute some private criterion, some transcendental mandate, for the processes of assimilation and concession, the ultimate product of which is law. The first fruits of a new social absolutism will not be more rights of Negroes or for anyone else, or even the immediate debauching of law, but rather the appearance of that all too-familiar irrationalism that muffles and strangles the clash of doctrines and impounds us all in dogma.

IV

POLITICS AND POSITIVISM

The fate of Newtonian physics warns us that there is a development of scientific first principles, and that their original forms can only be saved by interpretations of meaning and limitation of their field of application—interpretations and limitations unsuspected during the first period of successful employment. . . . Thus one aim of philosophy is to challenge the half-truths constituting the scientific first principles. The systematization of knowledge cannot be conducted in watertight compartments. All general truths condition each other; and the limits of their application cannot be adequately defined apart from their correlation by yet wider generalities.

—ALFRED NORTH WHITEHEAD [1]

A GLANCE AT the professional literature of politics of the past two decades reveals an atonishing percentage devoted to discussion of what sorts of things political scholars ought to be studying. One is sometimes tempted to wonder if all this preoccupation with the techniques of beginning do not mask a reluctance to "get on with it," to borrow a Britishism. In any case, much of this reflection is self-consciously ponderous and a smaller segment is slickly contrived to be noncommittal, but the principal motif is the continuing dialogue about how scientific the study of political phenomena can become, properly directed and nurtured. It would be a senseless cruelty to inflict upon the hopeful and conscientious reader one more pedantic essay advancing the claims and counterclaims of scientific methodology in the social sciences. Much of the undergrowth can be cut away by merely

1 *Process and Reality* (Humanities Press: New York, 1929), 15.

pointing out that the current quarrel results from the adoption by influential elements within professional political science of the spirit, if not the letter, of positivism. Should this be an accurate, if overly facile, description of the roots of political "behavioralism," then the less-discussed question of the impact of this orientation on present political realities can be undertaken with only minor detours.

Two "givens" can be expeditiously and mercifully assumed. One is the general outline of positivism itself (both "logical" and "garden variety") and the other is the methodically and tediously described position of the political behavioralists themselves—occupying foot after foot of shelf space and page after page in the journals of political technology. For those yet unbaptized, the encounter might well be made with any in a long list of positivistically committed "political scientists." Choose among them at random. David Easton, David Truman, or Robert Dahl are illustrious examples.

If this were a mere squabble among the academically fossilized, this intradisciplinary tilt between positivism and humanism in political science would be properly an object of sociological interest or mordant personal curiosity. But it is more than this. It is an intellectual engagement upon whose outcome rests the future development of political ideas and even the character of the national political life. However the political positivists have sought to disengage from the untidy scrapping of politics, they have in fact proven singularly influential, if only for the massive impact they have exerted on the rising generation of students of politics. The behavioralists are strongly ambivalent about this question of worldly influence. Priding themselves on scientific detachment, they announce that they seek to escape the trap of involvement with what behavioralist Richard Snyder calls "the 'real' world and 'concrete entities.'" Yet, there is more than a little evident longing for the gratifications of persuasion, a desire to whisper into the contrite ears of statesmen. In this passion, they are no different from all political thinkers since Plato dreamed of pulling the governmental wires in Syracuse. This craving for practical impact on affairs redeems the behavioralists; in this at least, they are really politicians after all.

While there are a number of critical defects in the general position put forward by political positivism, which shall be briefly described, I propose to argue that the claim of the behavioralists to dispassionate scientific objectivity is spurious, and that the total effect of positivism in this area has been to disastrously depress creative political thought and to contribute to the dangerous decline of ethical sensitivity in our political life.

The recommended perusal of positivistically generated political literature likely leaves the reader with a number of immediate reactions, even prior to the entertainment of more fundamental philosophic considerations. One of the curious features of contemporary political behavioralism is its admiration for operational concepts adopted from other disciplines, often without troubling to investigate rigorously their implicit philosophical problems, or even to determine whether the borrowed orientations are still currently viewed as being valid by the originating field of study. This situation is at once amusing and saddening; political science is very frequently cast in the role of a small-town literary society, discussing a novel already read, digested, and discarded in more cosmopolitan centers. With the breathless enthusiasm of a discoverer, behavioralism comes upon a new methodological device or a concept of science, but is too immersed in the joys of the quest to realize that the appropriated technique has already been retired as unsatisfactory. Sizeable elements of political science are still passing through the phase of naive positivism, antiquated academic psychology, and nineteenth century empiricism. Political scholars, filled with awe of the speculative physicist, still choose to live, paradoxically, in a world of Newtonian mechanics. Scientific method, beloved by social behavioralists, has undergone doctrinal revolutions as yet unassimilated by the would-be scientists of politics. One pertinent illustration is behavioralism's deep faith in quantitative measurement. But it has not kept abreast of developments in mathematics, and such developments point out to us that mathematics are not descriptive but are logical languages, constructable quite arbitrarily in infinite varieties of systems and in no way can they be shown to represent a correspondence with the "real" world of facts and objects, except insofar as mathematics can be used to hypothesize about relational sets. Beyond even this, contemporary physics has been confronted with a range of phenomena that defies quantitative analysis, and it courageously admits this and seeks to invent new approaches.

Another characteristic of behavioralism is its frenetic preoccupation with procedural problems rather than substantive questions. The behavioralists have developed a language for this; they speak of "research designs," "conceptual frames," and all manner of systems (including, incidentally, something labeled a "nulled system"). They are intensely concerned about the identification and delineation of the "discipline"—they are apparently most anxious not to be confused with philosophers and historians. "What is Political Science?" is a favorite gambit. The fastidiousness with which the behavioralists approach the problem of launching forth on investigation and study is matched only by the elaborate modesty which they affect regarding the possible fruits of their labors. Alas, much of the energy of contemporary political science is dissipated by unending discourse concerning the proprieties of commencing. If it were not a shady critical practice, one might be gravely enticed to speculate that this hyperanxiety over getting off on the right foot might have a certain psychological genesis. It is vastly more comfortable to busy oneself with the innocuous issues of methodology than to leap into the flood of alternative selection and recommendation. Regardless of how diligently circumspect the behavioralists may be in regard to observing the canons of proper scientific procedure, it would seem that their modesty might indeed have a certain justifiable and genuine quality. The gross product of thousands (doubtless, hundreds of thousands) of man-hours and dollars devoted to the study of politics is so spare of real significance as to be properly classified as an academic scandal. The most provocative work on politics has largely been done by philosophers, historians, sociologists, and even theologians, plus that tiny band of academic "untouchables" who still labor at humanistic political study under the aegis of departments of political science. Compared to the massive exertions of behavioralism, a Toqueville could more accurately find out what is going on by visiting a few saloons. Perhaps the oddest feature of political behavioralism is its failure to understand the nature of positivism. To a substantial degree, this inconsistency between sophisticated contemporary positivism and its offshoot, political behavioralism, stems from the proudly antiphilosophical inclinations of the social scientists. This disdain for philosophy is evident not only in the writings of the behavioralists, but also in their individual intellectual backgrounds and in the character of graduate study that spawned them and which they continue to promote. While positivism and pragmatism choose to renounce metaphysics, the political behavioralists elect to reject philosophy.

As we shall see farther on, this dismissal causes behavioralism to fall into some obvious entrapments, logical and axiological. Short of this, behavioralism's impatience with philosophic rectitudes renders it oblivious to some of the refinements of its progenitor, positivism. This is especially true in epistemological matters. The very least that can be said of contemporary positivism is that it has developed a mature regard for the problems of knowledge. But while political positivism assumes a commonsense realism of an unreflective variety, epistemologically speaking, positivism becomes preoccupied with the more subtle ramifications of phenomenalism.

The divergence of behavioral political science from its ideographic parent in such relatively abstruse matters as epistemology is not the crucial flaw in its *weltanschauung*. Far more serious is behavioralism's failure to grapple with three central problems, which for convenience we can label the ontological, scientific and psychological questions.

The political behavioralists would cheerfully renounce any predispositions toward ontological dogmatism; indeed, they would dismiss ontological discussion as a part of the metaphysical illusion, a suitable occupation for fanciful-minded professors of philosophy. Yet surely, they make, willy-nilly, a number of quite radical ontological assumptions. So does the much referred-to "man on the street," for that matter. But there is a significant difference between the ontological innocence of a busy insurance salesman and that of a social researcher. For example, whether or not ontic status ought to be accorded to nonexperientially cognized values may not much effect the functioning of the insurance salesman, but it does vitally impinge upon the researcher intent upon unraveling the root sources of human conduct. To decide what "is," to put it a bit brusquely, seems an elemental act prior to deciding what one might profitably investigate. This is a truism and, without question, social research, behavioral or otherwise, does proceed from some assumption as to the nature of being. The difficulty arises when the assumption is held without critical reflection, generally as a result of denying the necessity or validity of posing an initial ontological inquiry. This "loads" the question hopelessly. It forces subsequent research into a particular ontological frame by default; it also levels the complexity of ontological categorial analysis to a crude generality. It frequently gives rise to archaic mechanism and a simpleminded and discarded naturalism. The problem of ontological analysis with particular emphasis on the matter of categories and its relationship to social thought may well prove to be the most insistent task facing us.

Second, behavioralism seems enthralled with nineteenth century science. It relishes the simplicities of John Stuart Mill, but it appears confused and ill at ease about the nature of twentieth century science. If it is possible to generalize about the drift of contemporary science, separating it from mere technological innovation and refinement, it would seem that science has exchanged its empirical mood for mounting emphasis on logical analysis, for the rigorous examination of relationships between entities frequently hypothetical rather than categories of "pure actuality," and for a widening employment of mathematically grounded techniques of speculative investigation. The work of Eddington could be cited here as an apt example. Contemporary science is not simply placing nature under a microscope—this would be a most inadequate means of discovery. The vital ingredients of an analysis of natural life can be approached only by analysis of relatedness, varying effects of empirically nonverifiable entities upon each other. Thus, twentieth century science's view of nature is increasingly diverse, singularly unmechanistic and more rationally conceived. The demolition of some of the pristine simplicities of Newtonian mechanism is the classic case.

The ascendency of quantum physics is very much to the point here. The theories of Max Planck have not gone undeveloped by speculative physicists. Bohr, Hiesenberg, and Pauli, among others, have pursued the implications of Planck's revolutionary announcement that the energy emission of atoms is inconstant or "discontinuous." One major school of physical thought contends that the atom itself is immaterial, a category beyond the space-time continuum. In any case, the discontinuity apparent in quantum physics not only creates grave problems for the resolute materialists, but even revives the question of teleology. It has forced science to a consideration of "first principles" and even another look at Leibnitz and Spinoza. It has immeasurably complicated the more traditional view of nature, not only on the matter of immateriality, but also from the standpoint of intelligibility, categorealization, and hierarchy. Quantum physics has most certainly made a shambles of "pure" empiricism.

Third, behavioralism either chooses to chain itself to the obsolescences of academic psychology or, in a far more limited number of instances, to carve out of "depth psychology" certain attractive portions to be joined in a disconcertingly eclectic fashion to a number of social preconceptions. Both of these psychological postures are open to serious demurrer, whether the result is *The Structure of Society* [2] or *The Authoritarian Personality*.[3] One wise critic has commented that the real trouble with John Dewey's concept of personality was that he acted as though Freud had never existed. The political positivists well know that Freud existed (they are not so sure, one would gather, about Jung), but they choose to disregard a number of most fundamental and decisive doctrines of what can be loosely called "depth psychology." The most striking illustration of this is the silence behavioralists maintain regarding Freudian (or Jungian) concepts of the source and content of the unconscious and its formative role in the emergence of consciousness. In general, the behavioralists are suspicious of much emphasis on "unconscious" components in human personality, but they are shocked into virtually unbroken stillness by the proposition that unconscious content has its origins in part in extrapersonal sources. "Primal memory," the "collective unconscious," and similar ideas are divorced from behavioralist psychological conversation. Frequently, the behavioralists

2   Marion Levy, Jr., *The Structure of Society* (Princeton University Press: Princeton, 1952).

3   T. W. Adorno, et al, *The Authoritarian Personality*, (Harper: New York, 1950).

(and a few neo-Freudians, too) explain these precepts away by claiming that they are irrelevant to the general Freudian thesis. But this is a linguistic maneuver, accomplished at the price of doing violence to the underpinnings of Freudian thought. In the main, however, the behavioralists cling to the safer gunwales of experimental psychology and hail with gusto the behavior studies of pigeons, the surveys of the repetition of word usage among female factory employees, the interpersonal attitudes of postmen, and the "objective" testing of school children. This may all be well and even useful, but the behavioralists forget the contextual limitations of empirical psychology and the pitfalls which have already befallen reductionist tendencies in both academic psychology and psychologically related anthropology.

These lapses in adequacy can be traced to two main alternative causes. First, the behavioralists are unaware of the problems of ontology, are wholly ignorant of contemporary science, and have been unexposed to the implications of depth psychology. Second, they are not lacking in intellectual awareness, but for one reason or another, choose to ignore these issues or to pursue their inferences. It would be unthinkable to entertain proposition one; the ranks of American political science, with specific reference to the behavioral wing, contain too many capable and well-read scholars for this. The dialectical skill with which some behavioralists press their case belies any lack of exposure to intellectual currents, let alone insufficient analytical ability. It is proposition two that appears more promising. The deduction to be made from this proposition is that the reluctance of behavioral political science to face these problems arises more from ideological than philosophical causes. It is at this point that we can raise the issue of "value neutralism" and its reliability and effect on the vitality of present political thinking.

A few preliminary remarks may be in order. It is obvious

that the undertaking of any intellectual task involves certain "value" commitments. No one would argue that the very act of choosing what one proposes to investigate or analyze involves a selection from among possible objectives. All sorts of criteria can be constructed to validate this act of selection. Further, there must be some sort of standard of relevancy to appeal to in choosing the data or phenomena to be classified as material to the investigation. In one sense, these are value judgments, but this use of the term may stretch it a bit, at least out of the more axiological context we wish to establish. Let us, then, reserve the word "value" to apply to some sort of moral commitment, some variety of endorsement of right action, or validity of ethical judgment. It is when the term "value" is so defined that the behavioralists declare their neutralism from ethical bias.

It would be possible to attack the idea of value neutralism from a number of directions, quite apart from counterposing another ethic. It can be argued that the claim of being free from moral prejudice is fallacious, because while one might not be directly aware of formative moral conviction; such adherence does play, in fact, a significant role in the attitude and behavior of the individual. This argument can be refined in a number of directions, ranging from psychological analysis to mystic emergences. But we will let this argument go, engrossing as it might be.

The case against the behavioralist claim of moral neutralism must be put in other terms. At risk of approaching the matter in an overtly coy manner, we must suggest that the political positivists are really operating from a rather extensive ethical commitment, but one strictly *incognito*. Rather than being practitioners of value neutralism, the behavioralists have seriously endangered the validity of their entire approach to the study of politics by a stern and inflexible adherence to a latent value system. This is a considerable charge to level. It has been made with great cogency and eloquence by Leo Strauss in his essay appearing in *Essays on the Scientific Study of Politics,*[4] and an attempt will be made here not to parallel exactly Strauss's line of attack.

A careful scrutiny of contemporary activity in political science convinces that this is the only rational explanation. It is a conclusion arrived at after the lengthy process of discarding alternative hypotheses and culling from a formidable list of possible answers to the question: Why do the behavioralists hold with such tenacity to a number of dubious principles and refuse to take formal cognizance of the theoretical problems now besetting them?

What is this *incognito* value system that renders so much of American political science stubbornly doctrinaire? To answer this question requires an explanation of why political behavioralism shuns ethics in general, as well as certain specific philosophic, psychological, and scientific hypotheses. It is because behavioralism is almost pathologically hysteric about the resurgence of authoritarianism. This intense anxiety colors all that the political positivists produce. It forms their reactions to ethical discussion; it causes them to flee as from the plague any idea which appears to them likely to harbor any justification for political autocracy. This deep-seated fear, even compulsion, causes behavioralism to see bogeymen in the most unlikely places. Ethics itself is suspect; moral conviction becomes equated with sinister absolutism, itself a harbinger of political despotism. Even science, metaphysics, and psychology must not contain any indirect suggestions that point toward the revival of authoritarian social theory. The tragedy in all this is that the fears are of a rather paranoid sort, at least they are grossly exaggerated, and this hyperanxiety diminishes the sense of proportion required to perform useful intellectual work. In any case, the alternatives are not exhausted by behavioralism's *incognito* values on the one hand, and some horrid perversion of human society on the other. But even if that were the

4 "An Epilogue," in *Essays on the Scientific Study of Politics,* ed. H. J. Storing (Holt, Rinehart and Winston: New York, 1962), 307.

fact, if political positivism were really loyal to its scientific credo, it would face the eventualities with dispassionate calm. On the contrary, it elects to denigrate the historical discussion of value, while secretly indulging in vigorous moralism.

The value commitment of political positivism is to an uncompromising defense of egalitarianism, meliorism, and social atomism. Its active dedication is profound and unswerving. The degrees to which this creed is articulated vary among the behavioralists; the militancy tapers from Karl Popper or Harold Laswell to the less ideologically aroused. There are a priori propositions in the behavioralist world view, and they are emotionally entrenched convictions arising from the weight of cultural influence. The base tenets of popular democracy—majoritarianism, equalitarianism, the pragmatic dismissal of all aesthetic and moral judgments except the initial pragmatic one—are sacred writ. These *incognito* values, traveling under the false appellation of value neutralism, are often wedded to a Benthamite yen for reform, for behavioralists certainly are reformers at heart, so long as that reform is conducted within the scope of the prevailing cultural ideology.

Are these wrong values to espouse? This is indeed an open question, but we have a right as fellow hoemen in the vineyard to expect that such value orientations be in fact *espoused* (and presumably defended) if endorsed and that the question of the validity of the values remain open to interrogation. The depressing effect upon political thought resulting from an excess of political positivism is really the lack of candor presented by the artificialities of value neutralism and the attendant paralysis of political imagination prompted by the grimly doctrinaire attitudes of many political scientists. From an open intellectual society, we have been progressing toward a remarkably creedal one, under the guise of scientific detachment and ethical relativity. We face a new variety of intellectual orthodoxy in social thought. It is ironic, too, that the instigators of this limitation on speculation are themselves supposedly hostile toward "orthodoxy." But positivism—political or otherwise—has long ceased to be radical and now reposes in the benumbing sunlight of respectability. Man hankers after strange gods with unsettling frequency. One of the reasons that the twentieth century is such a perplexing epoch in which to live is not only the multiplication of these deities, but the shadow kingdoms where they are to be encountered.

V

RELIGION AND EDUCATION: THE BILL OF DIVORCEMENT

We can be content with no less than the old summary of educational ideal which has been current at any time from the dawn of our civilization. The essence of education is that it be religious.

Pray, what is religious education?

A religious education is an education which inculcates duty and reverence. Duty arises from our potential control over the course of events. Where attainable knowledge could have changed the issue, ignorance has the guilt of vice. And the foundation of reverence is this perception, that the present holds within itself the complete sum of existence, backwards and forwards, that whole amplitude of time, which is eternity.

—ALFRED NORTH WHITEHEAD [1]

ONE CANNOT HELP but sympathize with the enormous demands placed on the flexibility and ingenuity of public school administrators—a group not really notable for either quality—in the face of shifting constitutional interpretation by the Supreme Court. Since the public schools have been the main battleground for the clash of social theories and interests, these increasingly harried school bureaucrats have scarcely known from day to day just how they were to proceed in matters of basic school policy. They have adapted policy to racial integration and a variety of subsequent court directives in this area. More recently, the Court has made explicit the meaning of its conception of the separation of church and state.

1 *The Aims of Education,* Mentor Books (New American Library: New York, 1949), 26.

This explication is very likely incomplete at the present writing, and school boards and superintendents must entertain the probability of additional alterations of policy. But in at least one specific area, school administrators have found an admirable *modus vivendi*. To the question of the use of the Bible in the schools, they have responded with this simple test of legal legitimacy: If the Bible is used for purposes of literary or historical discussion its use is approved, but if it is used for purposes of worship or proselytization it is prohibited. What a happy and expedient solution.

But the fatal difficulty with this otherwise prudent arrangement is that it overlooks a fundamental area of Bible employment—and this situation, by extension, is illustrative of a major aspect of church-state separation in education which is overlooked and neglected. To explain: While it is obvious that the Bible is a source of literary and historical interest, and while it is equally apparent that it has and can be conceived of and used as a "holy book" in a sacramental sense (these two uses are relatively simple to identify), it is also the case that the Bible is a philosophic document. The Bible has been for centuries a source of *ideas* and these ideas are clearly neither exclusively literary-historical, eschatological, or sacramental. Now the question intrudes: How shall the Bible be treated in public schools as a source of philosophical discussion?

One answer might be that the public schools are no place for philosophical discussion or that such pedagogical enterprises are beyond the scope of educational programs in such schools, and that neatly takes care of that. I have no doubt that many people would believe this, and that there may be public schools which are utterly devoid of all serious discussion of ideas is a distinct possibility, although this latter situation would seem barely credible in the face of such announced activities as group discussions on "democracy versus communism," "marriage and the responsibilities of parenthood," "life adjustment," or the ethical ramifications of courtship practices and other weighty matters. To deny a certain philosophic content to these colloquies would seem unfounded.

If pressed, the indefatigible school administrator would more likely decide that the discussion of the Bible as a philosophic treatise—or religion in its philosophic aspects—was to be lumped together with its evangelical use and thereby to be banned. He should not be the object of either scorn or approbation for this decision, because it is not a personal one. The administrator might be a zealous Christian or a militant atheist, but he is simply facing the fact that the contemporary conception of the separation of church and state means not only the severance of a connection between formal religious practice and public education, but also the removal of religious philosophy as an underlying educational presupposition and as a legitimate educational undertaking.

What we are confronting is not one but two primary questions regarding the relationship of religion and education. The first one has been much debated, often with more vehemence and ruffled prejudice than with dispassionate reason. This question involves the place of religious worship in tax-supported institutions. Both religious worship and religious instruction construed to influence students toward religious affirmation, generalized or particularized, appear to violate the constitutional injunction against religious establishment. So be it, although this interpretation generates much opposition from church groups and there have been mutterings about constitutional amendments, now apparently dormant. In the same breath, major religious elements have either endorsed the view or have reconciled themselves to it, the principal source of continued dissatisfaction being some of the more fundamentalist Protestants.

By and large, the High Court's prohibitions seem reasonable enough when examined objectively. Stripped of legal technicality, the Court's reasoning appears thus: The United

States is not, in truth, a Christian state (as it formally declared itself, incidentally, in an early nineteenth century treaty with the Bey of Tunis). Its heterodox religious composition requires a position of absolute state neutrality; and to realize this, interpretation of church-state relations must entail the virtually complete withdrawal of state-supported activities that could be construed as either favoring religion in general or, by inference, any religious persuasion, Christianity or any of its fragmented sects.

For expedient reasons it could be expected that religious minorities would favor such a viewpoint, realizing that any state endorsement, overt or covert, would tend to give aid and comfort to the Protestant majority. The Catholics—or those Catholics who subscribe to this pragmatic thesis—do so with a heavy heart and a realization that it violates essential theological and social concepts. So, too, with many branches of more or less orthodox Protestants who support church-state separation. As for the nonreligionists, the present state of affairs is both gratifying and, to their notions, obvious and rational.

When viewed, not from the standpoint of denominational competition but in terms of the welfare of the commonweal, church-state separation in public institutions and education can be justified even by those whose personal commitment is to a theistic philosophy. The American public school, resting on a polyglot ideologic consensus, does not seem the appropriate milieu either for religious worship or catechismic pedagogy. Such undertakings appear more congenial with churches and households.

The second question is far more complex and has been relatively little examined: What is the relationship between religion and education not in institutional terms but philosophic ones? Does the formal separation of church and state in American public education mean the severance of a traditional bond between religion and humane learning, and if so, can it be tolerated?

In the paragraph above, I have alluded to a traditional bond. Putting aside the normative issue of any appeal to tradition, has such a bond existed, save in the cloisters of medieval universities? And even there, one might argue, was not the tie progressively parted, as at the University of Paris as early as the thirteenth century, for example? The formal liberation of philosophy from theology or the modern secularization of colleges and universities, previously and almost exclusively founded by religious bodies, is not tantamount to demonstrating that liberal education in the West has not rested upon theories of human nature and aspiration primarily Christian in origin and synthesis. Indeed, to go further afield, the intellectual endeavors of nonoccidental cultures have proceeded from foundations (both philosophical and institutional) of indigenous religions.

Historically the skein is not difficult to trace, from the Academy of Plato, founded on his aversion to the expedient vocationalism of the Sophists and his spiritualistic-ethical conception of education as individual and social self-realization, to Roman Stoicism and early Christian religious tutelage, to monastic reform and the rise of the universities, to the church-provided common schools, to the vast educational endeavors of the New World, in large part avowedly evangelical. Quite obviously it has not always been a harmonious relationship. Scientific inquiry was confused with heresy and muddied the waters, Erastian humanism shook it, Enlightenment skepticism and Rousseauistic primitivism damaged it, nineteenth century utilitarianism weakened the bond, and contemporary relativism has brought it to the brink of real separation.

The relationship of religion and education can be misunderstood even if one acknowledges its historic nature. The interrelatedness is not in content. A hermeneutic approach to education is not only unnecessary but undesirable. Education is not a supportive appendage to the religious enterprise, and educational content is not a reflection of shifting theological values or ought not to be. Rather, the traditional interconnection is moral, neither eschatological or soteriological. The significance and ultimate aim of education come from moral assumptions, and these have been amplified and promulgated, if not actually produced, in Western culture by Christianity. That the connection is ethical rather than formal can be deduced from an examination of those very disruptive tendencies mentioned in a previous paragraph. Until late in the nineteenth century, hostilities affecting the religious base of education were conducted *within* the arena of the religiously connected social institutions themselves, and the appearance of avowedly, even militantly, secular education appears almost simultaneously with the beginning of the breakdown of the hegemony of a social moral consensus resting upon principally Christian attitudes. Secularized education was a collateral offshoot of moral relativism; previous educational efforts, even when highly diversified, proceeded from the assumption of the existence of moral universals primarily as defined, at least in the popular sense, by Christianity.

This observation presents two parallel lines of argument: moral relativism versus moral absolutism, and, broadly, religiously grounded education versus secularized education. Thereby rests what might be viewed as an advantage of secular education: it is free to choose its own ethical orientations, it can select its own value base, relativistic or absolutistic. Christian-oriented education, conversely, cannot exercise that choice. This would seem a commendable liberty for secular education, but only so far as it could be demonstrated that the quality of the educational effort would be unaffected by the choice. If the qualitative aspect of education were significantly shaped by the selection of one or the other, then secular education would be at liberty to choose only in a Hobbesian sense of the word and the exercise of choice could be only described as perverse.

Neither would the choice be totally uninformed, since,

after all, the preceding educational practice had made the choice in favor of moral absolutism, and it would be necessary to make an appraisal of the desirability of this, assuming for the moment that secular education had no particular moral preconceptions.

The case for traditional, morally absolutistic education was not inconsiderable. Philosophy was written, cathedrals built, laws formulated, arts created, and so on, and these old glories were still about to be examined. Society was yet intact and man not wholly unrestrained. Overall, however, it is obvious that secular education felt the record unsatisfactory. Was this because it felt traditional education deficient in technique or morally fallacious or inadequate? With this question, we come full circle. It seems reasonable to infer that secularized education did not in fact freely choose between the moral alternatives, wishing to bicker with traditional education over pedagogical methodology, but, rather, its very genesis sprang from an a priori commitment to moral relativism.

To presume that moral relativism is the invariable ethical commitment of totally secularized education is not to contend that religiously oriented education is the only possible educational expression of a belief in moral absolutism. While the roots of comprehensively secular education are in the soil of relativism, an educational edifice could be constructed on a nonreligious base, still endorsing the viewpoint of the immutability of value. One could project a Kantian philosophy of education or one resting on the ethical opinions of Hartmann, Santayana, or G. E. Moore. But, with occasional exotic exceptions, educational systems are not built upon specific philosophical systems, but upon a wider base of cultural unanimity. This has meant in the West, for good or ill, that insofar as education was concerned, the claims of moral absolutism have been wholly identified with Christian theism.

In drawing the distinction between religious and secular

education, some cautions are in order. In this context, religious-oriented education is not to be confused with church schools or educational institutions operating on the basis of adherence to formal creeds, although so-called parochial institutions of learning are by no means excluded. By "secular," I choose to identify those institutions displaying no affinity with religious values or conceptions of human nature. It is not an easy line to establish, but it can be done if one does not confuse religious formalism with the vitality of religious philosophic values. In this light, the University of Chicago under Robert Maynard Hutchins, while hardly a parochial institution, was nonetheless profoundly oriented to religious values. In similar spirit, a private, nonchurch-affiliated liberal arts college may be in direct line of descent from the religiously developed ideals of Oxford and be quite pervasively Christian. On the other hand, numerous public and some private institutions of higher learning are secular in the fullest sense in that they have cut themselves adrift from the ethical tenets of religious tradition.

We may now be prepared for a crucial evaluative judgment set forth earlier in the essay. Does a continued reliance on religion, in a philosophic sense, violate the justifiable prohibitions regarding church-state separation in education? And even if it does, should it be abandoned?

To answer the first question in the affirmative would be to contend that the state could legitimately use its sanctions against ideas as well as practices. Religious philosophy scarcely appears as a seditious persuasion, although jokes have been made about public school pupils who "conspire" to pray, a levity which flies in the face of any informed understanding of the Court's recent dicta. A prohibition against religious practices, then, is not a fiat against religious values and it seems to me there need be no anxiety that the restraint of one will be the demise of the other. A good argument could be made to the contrary, that religious practices as doubtless executed in state-supported institutions would lessen the acceptance of religious values rather than enhance them. Regardless of one's liturgical predilections, the so-called "Regents' Prayer" that provoked *Engels* v. *Vitale* was a thoroughly dismal piece of rhetoric, and, its theological opaqueness aside, would hardly promote reverence or piety.

Education seems free to go its own way regarding the acceptance or rejection of its traditional religious inspiration and ethical values, and the question of resistance to state intervention in this matter appears academic. The real question is what education *ought* to do. The case for "religious education" can be made, I think, on three principal grounds: (1) Education in order to perform its amelioratory individual and social function must maintain its historic ethical base; education resting on moral relativism is virtually a contradiction in terms. (2) The progress of secularization in education means the retreat of theology as a forceful and respectable intellectual inquiry. (3) Religious education must be preserved in order to effect vital social controls and individual restraints, to inculcate "duty and reverence" (to reiterate Whitehead's phrase).

Education without ethical sanction must presume egocentric education. If one asks why educate anybody, and one initially discards the traditional absolutistic ethical justification, there are three conceivable responses. Either the process of acquiring the education itself provides some variety of individual gratification; or that education enables one to attain some subjectively designated ends—money, status, security; or education is necessary for the survival of the state in that it provides training needed for defense and the maintenance of domestic services.

The issue, of course, is whether these nonethical justifications are adequate; it is apparent that they are important factors not to be summarily dismissed. It is perfectly reasonable to assume that the educational process itself may be and even should be personally gratifying. Education as a means of furthering one's purposes, developing one's talents or skills, is warrantable and even praiseworthy. Certainly the security and prosperity of the state are impelling reasons for educational endeavor. But the point to be made is that these factors not only are not central to education, but, if conceived as primary, can be both debilitating and pernicious.

The question of education for subjective satisfaction hinges upon a concept of human nature. Aristotle makes a telling case in the *Nicomachean Ethics* for education as personal satisfaction, peremptorily dismissing other motives, even social service. But Aristotle assumes man to be both a moral entity and a "social animal." Education as personal gratification meant for him self-realization, defined not only in moral terms, but also without a radical distinction between individual moral fulfillment and social involvement.

If one conceives the nature of the person in non-Aristotelian terms (or non-Christian terms) and embraces naturalistic and reductionistic definitions, seeing man as either a mobile digestive system or a melange of imperious instinctual drives, then the idea of personal gratification takes on a vastly different character. Whatever else education may be in this view, it is not categorically different from a host of other activities, e.g., nourishment, sex, amusement; and the choice of education as gratification becomes a matter of subjective preference based on some scale of felt sublimations. In these terms, education must inevitably be reduced to diversion or therapy in the catharsis sense. Of course, it would in so doing not only be divested of its ethical component, but its intellectual one as well. No scale of analytic priorities could be established between physics and square-dancing, philosophy or interior decorating. I submit that the secularization of education has already proceeded to the point where this same state of affairs is beginning to be revealed.

The second justification for nonethical education is old and well known: education is a means to self-designated ends, and these ends can be broadly classified as status goals, since they are invariably connected with wealth, vocational respectability, public influence, professional prestige, social acceptance, and class identifications. This is not only the underlining of pragmatism, but is, perhaps, the *raison d'etre* of mass public education. The college degree becomes a union card, a passport to social mobility, or a certificate of social acceptability. There can be no doubt that educational experience is utilitarian in this way. College graduates make more money than noncollege persons, middle-class vocations and professions require higher education, political leadership becomes increasingly identified with at least moderate educational qualification. Educational testimonials are more generally a requirement for attaining even lower middle-class respectability, particularly as college matriculation is becoming available to all who exhibit some mild interest in it.

When all this is admitted, one still feels inclined to pose the rather rudimentary question: Is society better off as a result and are individuals happier? I would be among the last to disparage the social benefits of education *qua* education, but education envisioned in this particular manner raises some vexing problems. Education for status runs into the obstacle that status is always relative; my status is defined and enhanced in relation to someone else's, and this sort of educational motivation creates an accelerating upward spiral in which a satisfactory level cannot be reached because such a level cannot be stationary. The status "ante" is always being "upped." This is true in terms of the acquisition of material symbols, professional position, and even academic degrees. Too many people hold baccalaureate degrees, so a master's degree must be had in insure status, but this also is too common and the doctorate must be sought (although some institutions, I understand, have created a degree they call "Educational Specialist" to provide status for public school teachers who wish to rise above the ignominy of the master's). I am inclined to think that sooner or later we must establish a formal postdoctoral degree of some kind to meet the needs of advancing status.

Ironically, education for status creates a form of educational snobbery far more virulent than the more traditional type. The fact remains that there are a multitude of vital, honorable, and significant services to be performed for society that do not require a college degree. And to suggest that these vocations are beneath the consideration of young people is a cruel slander against those who labor in this way, is socially disruptive, and tends to persuade people naturally drawn to these activities, who might find in them contentment and fulfillment for their skills, to hold back because of artificial and snobbish status indoctrination. To place a higher education requirement on these jobs would be utterly foolish and wasteful. I find really knowledgeable and efficient automobile repairmen a great rarity; they are immensely useful and I have an intense dependence on them and admiration for their skills. But I care not a whit if they hold B.A. degrees or M.Sc. degrees or are "Doctors of Motors." I don't think society should care either, although I venture society might take a lively interest in whether they were moral men, good parents, responsible citizens and, in general, humane human beings.

It is questionable whether education for status has had any noticeable civilizing effect on the social order. It would surely be a *post hoc* argument to trace the contemporary malaise to this source, on the other hand. But two observations seem fair. First, the growth of this educational precept has not had any perceivable influence in curbing the increase of antisocial patterns of behavior well catalogued by sociological investigation. Whether it has contributed to them is debatable. Second, there is evidence that youth itself is beginning to rebel against the "education for status" doctrine. This educational notion seems a last vestige of social darwinism, a pragmatic rearrangement of nineteenth century neo-Calvinism, the final epilegomenon of the soap-opera "American dream." And youth, in a sort of baroque high dudgeon, is in open revolt.

Why? Because the frenetic chase for status, to which secularized education has been a major contributor, has not made people nearly as happy as had been advertised. On the contrary, it has left them frustrated, prone to neurosis and nihilism, has invited them to entertain as replacement bizarre mysticisms, and a sort of sullen, sensuous epicureanism. It has also provoked, *mutas mutandis,* a variety of moral hunger, compellingly engaging in its very intensity and naivete when the posturings of adolescence are stripped away. Contemporary youth is neither happy nor whole, but one suspects that they are closer to being so by dint of a stimulus to inquiry than their often ideologically mesmerized and ethically bankrupt pedagogues. The sins of exploration are always less appalling than those of fanaticism.

Can education rest upon service to the state? One might hastily reply that Plato or Hegel thought so, but they did so by endorsing a view of the state drastically different from our own. We do not live under the aegis of the *polis,* idealized or otherwise, nor under the reign of the Absolute, both conceptions of the state similar to the degree that individual and corporate destinies were inextricably intertwined and these fused purposes were ethical in nature. When we deny the spiritual or even rational origins of the state, we must deny, too, the premise that the purpose of education is the support of the state. If the state is an artificial human contrivance, created to perform necessary social tasks, we assume that the ultimate social end is something beyond the existence and promotion of the state. What this "something" may be—individual well-being or the collective good—is problematical given the initial premise, but its existence demonstrates that the education of men can be only in part concerned with the needs of the state. The greater part must be devoted to pursuit of the end for which the state itself was created.

In less abstruse terms, it is not difficult to imagine the reaction of the nominally libertarian American to the full ramifications of the assertion that education rests on service to the state. While he might be willing to admit that the state is justified in promoting its own defense and enhancing domestic well-being and that it clearly utilizes the skills and knowledges of its citizens to these purposes, he recoils from the extant example of the statist principle in action—education in the Soviet Union. Even the obvious accomplishments of this system in science and technology do not prompt him to subscribe to it, although he may and has been tempted to adapt certain emphases from it in order, he supposes, to be competitive in the race for technological efficiency. Aside from his rejection of the monolithic concept of the state, the American is further repulsed by the Soviet system because he still vaguely believes that education has something to do with individual development and happiness (which entails certain individual choices) and that the whole procedure somehow involves moral issues not definable in terms of the self-proclaimed purposes of the state. Even if the American leans toward a more collectivist view, he denies the identity of the state with society and conceptualizes education as being socially supportive rather than ancillary to the state.

To reject a philosophy of education emanating from individual gratification, status desire, or state service is to reject a nonethical conception of education or education based upon individual moral relativism. We might even be prepared to argue that to use the word "education" in the above context is contradictory. But it could be vigorously contended that even if the contrary is assumed—that education must rest on moral values—this moral base need not be absolutistic or religious. If not these, what? The broad reply would be the defense of cultural relativism. True, the cultural relativist would argue, education rests on something other than individual preference, but this moral substructure of education is neither a collection of moral universals nor a religious metaphysic, but rather a set of culturally evolved social rules and values. Education is built upon and reflects these social canons, so the argument goes.

It is beyond the scope of this discussion to analyze or refute the claims of the cultural relativists in general, but certain doubts could be expressed as to the tenability of this position in its relation to education. First, there is the matter of the adequacy of cultural relativism's account of the origins or manifestations of moral consciousness and ensuing judgments within a given culture. To assume that moral consciousness is either reducible to historical accident or environment stimulation and response seems dubious and incapable of explaining the full range of ethical phenomena. This explanation is no more satisfying on logical grounds than the doctrine of evolutionary "emergences." To the contrary, there appears a viable ubiquity in moral awareness and practice from one culture to another. More specifically, there is evidenced a marked universality of trans-cultural values in the educational process itself. Particularly in the West, the value systems presupposed in the educational efforts of diverse cultures, European and American, have, at least in part, displayed a remarkable similarity. Finally, the critical flaw in a culturally relativistic ethic for education is the problem of ascertaining just what constitutes an autonomous culture insofar as a value base for education is concerned. Should we have something called "American education" and "Canadian education" and "Burmese education"? What ought the differences to be and how significant are they? The corollary of this problem is even more disturbing. If one defines the value base of education in cultural terms, then education is clearly restricted to the limits drawn by cultural prescription, and the culturally self-analytical and self-critical function of education is denied. Also denied is the transcultural community of intellectual endeavor, except in terms of the exchange of technological data or folk lore and, in consequence, education becomes not an inquisitive and liberating process, but one dedicated to the preservation of cultural mores and social idiosyncrasies. A microcosmic illustration of this deleterious doctrine is the American public school, its vigor and imagination sapped by the pressures upon it to enforce highly localized customs and prejudices. Education must recognize and promote values, but these must be conceived in a more expansive and lofty shape than provincial preferences, national vanities, and even cultural *folkgeists*.

What is left is what we have called "religious education." This conception of education stands on three fundamental principles: (1) Man is a spiritual, moral, and aesthetic being, and education is concerned with the process of developing the individual capabilities of these facets of human nature. While primary attention is given to the training of the intellect (man being an integrated organism), the intellectual cannot be developed in isolation from the spiritual, moral, and aesthetic. (2) Moral values exist external to human reason, but are accessible to rational discovery, as, indeed, is our universe to our sensual perceptions. Man, while free, is obliged both to recognize and to obey these moral values and to employ his reason to discover the nature of his environment. Education proceeds from this assumption and toward this goal. (3) As man lives not in isolation, either metaphysically, morally, or socially, he is bound by duties, among which are reverence, obedience, rational investigation, and reciprocal social service. The purpose of education is to foster reverence, inculcate duty, liberate and refine rational investigation, and further human social welfare and happiness.

This is scarcely a novel or even unexpected statement—it "has been current at any time from the dawn of our civilization." Its persuasiveness arises not from its novelty, but from its continuity. But it is a continuity threatened by the secularization of education. The preceding description of educational purpose is not specifically a Christian one; I know numerous non-Christian persons who would subscribe to it, and I know a number of Christians, for that matter, who would not, inexplicably, altogether subscribe to it, but I think these individuals are religious men and women. In like spirit, I would not argue that education ought to produce Christians. That is not the function of education, but rather of the church in our scheme of the division of labor. But that the statement above is a religious one is difficult to doubt. And if the aim of education is the fulfillment of men's intellectual, spiritual, moral, and aesthetic potentialities, it is a religious undertaking.

The separation of religion and education in a philosophic (and certainly in a formal) sense would denigrate the significance and even the institutional status of theology. I for one would regret seeing theology banished to the seminaries; so would most fair-minded agnostics I know and a large portion of them are. The relegation of theology to totally denominational auspices would have an unwholesome effect on theology, but even its limitation to the upper air of graduate schools of religion would be lamentable. Whether or not it provokes elation or despair or mere indifference, it is an undeniable fact that the current undergraduate population displays a prodigious religious illiteracy. This fact need not necessarily stimulate any evangelical fervor, and I would vehemently oppose using educational institutions for such purposes, except insofar as religious groups seek to compete in the general marketplace of ideas outside the official structure of the university. But the cause of religious literacy should find a sympathetic hearing among all those who presume to endorse liberal education. The disregard of this sector of intellectual awareness seems arbitrary in view of the immeasurable influence it has exerted on Western civilization. Fear concerning violation of church-state *apartheid* ought not to cause us to place an interdict over an entire traditional area of learning.

Theology has a place, therefore, in the basic learnings as well as in the more speculative areas of scholarship. But when the term "theology" is used to refer to the undergraduate curriculum, its meaning should be specified with some care. In the first place, it should refer to what loosely could be described as the history of religion, to include its ethical, political, social, and artistic influences, as well as its own historical development. In this connection, it would seem desirable that a college graduate ought to be reasonably familiar with the contents of the Old and New Testaments, the main outlines of church history, the major tenets of the dominant religions of the world, and the principal branches of Christendom.

Second, theology should be thought of in terms of religious philosophy. While no institutional preferential treatment is due, religious philosophy certainly deserves an attention commensurate with its influence and credibility. If one has little enthusiasm for officially sanctioned evangelism, and I am such a person, one ought to have a corresponding disquietude regarding the exclusion of religious thought from the curriculum on equally ideologically centered grounds. If our aim is to instill a questioning cast of mind and to refine powers of intellectual discrimination, then, in extension, those powers should be used over the full range of human speculation.

In the larger community of scholars, theology remains an indispensable intellectual enterprise, despite the idiocies frequently produced under its *imprimatur*. Antitheological scoffers relish pointing out these embarrassing gaucheries, often forgetting the rational lapses now and again coming to light in such presumably more disciplined and empiric areas as biology, psychology, or anthropology. Philosophy has had its ravings, too, and even its hoaxes (if Bertrand Russell is to be believed) and, in the main, professional philosophers accept these with estimable good grace and even humour. It is true that often theologians tend to be dreary and self-opinionated fellows, occasionally tempted to replace rational argument with internally received dicta from on high. But even philosophers can be accused of this, as Santayana once indicted Kant by saying that his ethical theories were ". . . fossils, found unaccountably imbedded in the old man's mind, he regarded as evidences of an inward but supernatural revelation."

The reputation of theology is often impugned by those whose positivistic conditioning causes them to draw no distinction between revivalistic inanities or Pealean rubbish and serious contemporary theological inquiry. They are not to be too strenuously blamed, however, considering that many self-announced religionists cannot perform a similar bit of surgery. In certain quarters, Ockham's Razor is a neglected tool.

The theological dialogue has been unusually spritely in the post-World War II era, and its repercussions have been suggestively felt in axiological philosophy and social theory. It would be most regrettable if educational secularization would tend to exile this provocative realm of insight and controversy and bar it from the general intellectual colloquy. The scholastic life would be made markedly the poorer for it; and theology itself would be injured if for no other reason than the probable discouragement of fertile and sophisticated minds from indulging in it, leaving that noble art in the hands of sterile simplifiers and academic faith healers.

The terms "reverence" and "duty" carry negative connotations in our society. They are occasionally heard from the pulpit or political rostrum, but their employment is meant to be innocuous since their deeper emotive effect is to provoke hostility in the popular mind. Reverence appears to suggest either obsequiousness or sanctimony, or both; duty implies the recognition of some authority and a corresponding individual restraint and subordination of choice. To a society basically secular, egalitarian, and egocentric, reverence and duty seem to smack of a feudal age when individual man was neither his own master nor his own theologian.

The individualistic freedom of our century is, to some extent, illusory. Duties remain and may have even multiplied. The life of the individual man is far more regulated by distant authorities of the state, the corporation, the organization than it previously has been and surely this control represents assignment of duties. That a man does not consciously think of these obligations as duties merely indicates his relinquishment of the idea that the performance of these duties is an act of his will. He discharges these duties either because he understands and fears the punitive consequences of disobedience, or he has been convinced that the performance of duties is in his direct self-interest and, therefore, they are not *really* duties but "opportunities." He does not feel bound by a code to which he is personally and uniquely accountable.

Further, these duties are not only thought of as being something other than personal recognition and acquiescence, but they represent demands on man that are superficial and ephemeral because they are neither concerned with man's essential nature nor his basic relationships. What is clearly lacking is love and it is love that redeems duty from sterile poverty and crushing mechanism. How can a man love a government, or an insurance company, or a factory, or Rotary International? The absence of love and the absence of the recognition of the objects of love cause men to talk nervously about freedom, while becoming increasingly burdened with regulation, performing social chores without the compensation of deep satisfaction or moral peace. Historically, notions about freedom have varied, but two main concepts have come to the fore and they have vied with each other for ascendency. One describes freedom as an absence of restraint upon action and choice, or freedom as action and choice unrestrained save when it directly intrudes on the actions and choices of others.

The other viewpoint supposes freedom to consist of the performance of duty. This cold, blunt definition strikes contemporary Americans as abhorrent. Is this not, they reflect, the premise of totalitarianism? It has been so employed, but the alternative idea of freedom has been put to use by antidemocrats, too, such as savage jacobinism. The theoretical dispute over the merits of these two definitions need not occupy us here. The inferences to be drawn from the juxtaposition of them is that freedom conceived solely as unrestricted activity seems inadequate, or at least is an inaccurate description of our present state of affairs; and any concept of freedom involving the matter of duty must provide some morally satisfactory explanation for the origin, nature, and characteristics of obligations and duties.

The contemporary American knows, perhaps subconsciously, that he does not possess the freedom of the first definition and, at the same time, he finds little fulfillment in his duties, little freedom. The point he has missed is that the nature of duty is moral and not societal, that duties are reciprocal and are amalgamated by love. In this concept, a man performing his moral duty can anticipate some very palpable returns, of which happiness can even be extended as a probable result. But the process of discovering and identifying moral duty is rational not visceral. A man cannot do this alone in a sort of romantic frenzy, perceiving moral truth in a flashing intuition to the accompaniment of lightning and cyclonic winds. He finds it by the calmer processes of reason and in this venture he needs aid and direction.

One might hazard the observation that historical and anthropological research seems to show that men everywhere seek some object of reverence. The objects obviously vary and the yearning to revere can be explained on a number of levels from the supernatural to the psychological. Gods, animals, kings, heroes, nations, symbols, bank accounts, and dunghills have all been the objects of reverence at one time or another with varying results. But consider for a moment what we have done. God is dead (even some theologians now espouse this idea); totemism is dead; the king is dead; we have more or less dispensed with the hero except as political manipulator and satyr; nationalism is dying, except among the newly-liberated primitives; symbols have been shorn of their magic by analysis; bank accounts have lost their mystique; dunghills are not adaptable to an urbanized culture.

The end-product is a void, felt as a psychic craving and sufficiently intolerable that we have struck upon the one replacement left—we will revere ourselves. Put a trifle less epigrammatically, we have enshrined the human psyche itself as our object of reverence. Our developing social and political thought undeniably discloses this, and a comprehensive examination of the phenomenon would entail an impossibly lengthy digression. But the social results can be identified more summarily. We are becoming a society of narcissists; tense vanity reigns and we have made a cult of egocentricity, exhaustively rationalizing this self-flattering conception with ideologically slanted empiricism. The perils of egocentricity have long since been carefully described from Plato and Augustine through the development of Christian doctrine and social theory permeated by Christian philosophy. The phenomenon of mass egotism is contemporary, but the outcome has long been predicted. I see no present basis for rejecting this prognostication.

Education, if it is in truth education, must be in the business of helping men to find what they may initially lack—a recognition of moral duty and an enduring object of reverence. True education does this in two ways. First, it plays a conserving and perpetuating role, maintaining unbroken the continuity of man's thought, values, aesthetic longing and creation. Man is the only creature of nature who constructs anything designed to serve more than his immediate interests; he builds cathedrals knowing he may not live to see them completed, he writes symphonies without the positive knowledge he will hear them performed, he explores nature aware that his discoveries may be partial and inconclusive without the additional contributions of those who will postdate him. Education keeps their skein intact, primarily by teaching men that a prime moral duty involves individual participation in transepochal transference of values and wisdoms. This can be called "covenantal education" and its core is reverential, the antithesis of egocentricity.

Second, education trains men in moral judgment, in ethical discriminaton. It aids men in the process of selectivity of substantial moral values and duties from spurious enthusiasms and merchandized passions. Much has been made of Mr. Norman Vincent Peale's proclamation of the "power of positive thinking" and much of it, to me, is pseudo-kerygmatic pomposity and sly utilitarianism, but, in any case, the moral function of education may be *positive* in purpose, but *negative* in technique. Education extolls the "power of negative thinking," and intelligent, disciplined skepticism among those who are capable of it is one of morality and religion's best allies. There is no denying that education must presuppose a sort of gnosticism in which it recognizes that certain institutions of social control effect ethical restraint by dint of bald authority and persuasive appeal. But for those who are prepared to experience higher education, the individual moral encounter is far more fluid. Intellectual discipline supersedes extrinsic kinds, and reflection is quite as much concerned with what ought to be discarded as with what ought to be preserved. This implicit separation is not an either/or proposition. No men, save the mentally incompetent or morally depraved, can find moral fulfillment exclusively either by external directives or the impress of social institutions. No sophisticated intellect can acquire the same resolution of his moral quandary in total solitude or by totally dialectical means. Nonetheless, institutionalized education in its role of a moral agency recognizes a difference in technique and orientation from the moral instruction of family, church, and state. To some, therefore (doubtless a minority), the moral agency of education is far more formative than these other social organs. Moreover, much of the vitality, the rejuvenating *élan* of the social ethic is traced to the intellectualism of education.

In sum, the separation of religion and education would foster the eventual perishing of the latter, its substitute being a hyperorganized but arid reflection of the transient prejudices and social vanities of daily existence. Education aims at deepening the religiosity of life, not by sacramental emphasis in the strict use of that phrase, but by the reiteration of the significance of the transtemporal, what is above and below, what is past and what is future.

VI

THE ARTIST
AS ACADEMICIAN

IF ONE STROLLED along the streets on the Left Bank in the twenties or thirties, he would not have found it difficult to compile an imposing catalogue of artists of all sorts—painters, poets, novelists, composers—most of them not French by birth, most of them transplanted from their native climes to the possibly more congenial atmosphere of Paris—Joyce, Miller, Hemingway, Cummings, Durrell, Stein, many others. Look for them now and you will not see them, at least not in any such concentrated numbers. The current smaller crop of expatriates is scattered—the Costa Brava, Mexico, the south of France, the Caribbean, and even in chilly Britain. They are only a few in comparison, perhaps even less significant in artistic impact.

Where have they all gone? Where should one look now? Since World War II, the migration of the artistically productive has not been directed toward exotic retreats but into the sanctuary of the university. The artist has accepted the bread and lodging of the academic and, *en masse*, he has settled, more or less gracefully, into the routine of the professional academic. Hardly a major university exists that does not boast of at least one publicly acclaimed creative artist; even smaller and less-renowned institutions invariably include at least one or two practicing talents who meet the definition of "artist." This is at once a singular and quite intriguing situation; on the surface at least, a happy arrangement, far better perhaps, than capricious private patronage or obtuse public subsidization. However sanguine the picture may appear at first glance, the academic underwriting of art—or more pointedly the combining of function of artist and academician—raises a complex of unsettling questions, some of them touching upon the health of creative endeavor in general, the relation of art and artists to the community (both in its academic and broader sense), and the effect of pedagogical labor, however limited, upon the individual artist. These reflections *in toto* provoke the inference that the university employment of creative artists may not be quite the halcyon solution of an age-old problem that it first appears to be, or that the entire arrangement demands the sensitive adjustment and perceptive forbearance of all concerned.

It may be to the point to settle first upon a working definition of art in order to classify those who are its practitioners. I am not so rash as to pretend that we can proceed with any definitive conception of art, but a useful generality is perhaps possible.[1] Art is a formulation into disciplined activity of two human capacities: the ability to encompass the full range of the objective world, "public" and "private," and the ability to recreate those objects in a system of symbolic forms. I argue that these capabilities are at once the qualities that distinguish the civilized man from the primal horde, and also are the qualities constitutive of what we call the aesthetic mode of response, discovery and response. To the artist, this aesthetic mode of dealing with experience is something more than a subsidiary increment in his emotional and intellectual engagement—it is the starting point, the *raison d'etre,* the pervading, even compulsive, orientation. Nor is this aesthetic concern a neurotic compensation, a rechanneling of imperious libido, as some neo-Romantics would have us believe. Neither is this essential aesthetic discovery and response for the artist the pursuit of knowledge. It is with this basic consideration—the confusion

1   My conception and definition of art is strongly influenced by Eliseo Vivas. See his "Art and the Artist's Citizenship in *The New Argument in Economics,* ed. H. Schoeck and J. W. Wiggins (Van Nostrand: Princeton, 1963). See also Vivas' *The Artistic Transaction* (Ohio State University Press: Columbus, 1963), especially Part 1.

of art and knowledge—that the schism between artist and academic becomes apparent.

When one stops to think about it, this is a common confusion. Art is generally believed to convey "great truths" and the implication is that this is done in a quite didactic way. Albert Schweitzer has been quoted as saying that "the dogma of the Trinity can be expressed more clearly and satisfactorily in music than in verbal formulae." [2] This is highly doubtful, to say the least, principally because the statement misinterprets the nature of musical communication. It is one thing to argue that music creates in the listener a mood of noumenal receptivity, quite another that it either seeks or accomplishes the discursive examination of religious or philosophical truth. [3]

Taken from another direction, the contention that art is but another medium for the dissemination of knowledge results in the frantic efforts of our self-appointed artistic censors, the latter-day moral inquisitors among us, who are convinced that art is predominantly nurtured by the demonic or dionysian and expresses a potent but traducing ideology. The supposition that art is imbued with knowledge of the sort encountered in other areas of human productivity gives birth to two major and intimately related problems, a confusion between art and education [4] and, hence, a confusion between the roles of the artist and the academician; and the popular notions about the value of art.

No one can doubt that the public takes education seriously; whether seriously enough, or what might be the real roots of its concern regarding education, are provocative speculations. But these may not be germane here. Because art is thought of as being an educational adjunct, it is re-

2 As quoted by Vivas in "Art and the Artist's Citizenship," 217 [from Cecil Gray's *History of Music* (Knopf: New York, 1931), 270.].
3 For a fuller discussion, see Eliseo Vivas' "Literature and Ideology," in *The Artistic Transaction*, 95.
4 For a particularly provocative elaboration of this confusion, see Eliseo Vivas' "Art and the Artist's Citizenship."

garded as vaguely valuable, a desirable cultural attribute, a personal adornment, even a status symbol if not pursued with unseemly vigor. Art can be merchandised like popular education.

This attitude wholly denigrates the nature of art, rendering it trivial and in no way an imperative factor in the radical determinations of human thought and conduct. The fact is that the public does not take art seriously—to what extent this point of view is shared by academic communities is a matter with which we shall deal later.

What is clear is that art is something at once more *and* less than the popular conception of it. It is *not* a vehicle for the conveyance of conceptually framed statements or rational propositions. It *is* an attempt to reconstruct symbolically the universe and human experience by individual disengagement through the suppression of subjective urges and demands. Art goes beyond perception and observation in that the artist goes beyond discovery to invention, the injection of novelty, the reordering of symbols into systematic unities. Thus, art's role becomes the means by which man comes into contact with both the inner core and outer covering of experience.

The artist, then, is one whose essential approach is in the aesthetic mode, his basic involvement being with this symbolic constitutive activity. The division of labor is clearly implied; the roles of the artist and of the academic are separate, the latter concerned with the discovery of cognate truth. This does not altogether resolve our difficulty, especially as the artist increasingly becomes a wearer of the academic mantle. Are the two roles compatible, either from the standpoint of these most fundamental *weltanschauungen,* or even on the basis of institutional and personal practicability? Surely the title of this essay implies the hierarchy— is a man to be an artist as academician or an academician as artist? Inevitably a choice must be made. Admitting for the moment at least that a reconciliation is possible, there can be only one prime commitment—the individual must first be dedicated to the production of art, or he must be similarly devoted to academic scholarship. Indeed, one may beautifully enhance the other, but the root approach to the reception of experience can never be in exact balance; it would be a vain equilibrium. One cannot serve two masters without hopeless delusion. There remains, however, the question of cross-fertilization between the aesthetic and cognitive insights.

At least, we can answer the question of who *is* the artist? We can define him, on or off a university campus, as a creative individual whose primary commitment is to the aesthetic mode, who attempts to cope subjectively and cogently with reality and experience in terms of symbolic form. We can now begin to look at the artist and his art within his newly adopted environment—the university— and examine his peculiar problems. What is his role in this community? Does it differ from his ordinary social role? Are there reciprocal advantages to the artist and the university? What is the effect on creativity of academic employment? Is there an artistic freedom beyond academic freedom? What is the relationship between the production of art and teaching? Does the academic community and the general public really wish to support the production of art on art's own terms?

It must be freely acknowledged that the employment of celebrated writers, poets, sculptors, painters, composers, and certain performing artists (such as dancers and solo musicians) whose interpretative skills are clearly creative represents a variety of subsidization. It might be attractive to consider that these people "pay their way" by giving an annual lecture, talking poetry with a select circle of students now and again, or criticizing a yearly student art show. But, in truth, this would be stretching a point. Beyond the so-called "artist-in-residence" arrangement, there are numerous

artists who perform nearly full-time academic duties and at
the same time produce what we may call "public art," that is,
publicly available work either as writers, musicians, or plas-
tic artists. This, too, is subsidization in that virtually every
enlightened institution reduces normal academic loads for
its producing artists; beyond this, all working artists historically have earned their bread—from designing military for-
tifications to composing public odes and court masques. The
university pays the artist for services rendered, but this indirectly subsidizes his art and this is clearly understood—no
university president today would seriously suggest docking
a faculty member's pay because his symphony was com-
posed on "university time."

Unavoidably, art must be subsidized. History does not
reveal a period when art "paid for itself." It must be subsidized because it is never really popular, never really of
sufficient value in the marketplace to be universally supported. Certain isolated examples of art can be cited as
moneymaking enterprises, but the incidents are too infrequent to support the entire undertaking. For every Alfred
Lord Tennyson there are ten Gerard Manley Hopkinses, as it
were. The forms of subsidization range from the wealthy
aristocratic patron, to the individual philanthropist, to the
private foundation, to government. This is not the time to
enter into this controversial arena, except to add that in my
view there is something to be said for the maligned private
patron, Lord Chesterfield notwithstanding, and there is
nothing but artistic disaster in the forms of state subsidization now being widely discussed. This form of paying the
bill for "culture" really means bureaucratization, and this
means the final reign of the philistines. Philistines are always
to be endured, but the idea of governmental philistines con-
trolling governmental funds and becoming public arbiters of
art is too alarming to be lightly dismissed.

Be that as it may, the subsidization of art by ostensibly
humane institutions of higher learning may be the lesser of

several evils. I am convinced that it is far less an evil than governmental organization of the arts, not because I think that government arbitrarily means ideological conformity, but because almost invariably government means the suppression of the creative imagination in favor of publicly endorsed mediocrity. There are, however, pitfalls in the university method as well, and one of them is that it may provide a retreat for the artist that is far too comfortable in terms of a stylized mode of living. The salient argument of the governmental-subsidy advocates is, bluntly, that artists, too, ought to enjoy the fruits of the affluent society. Many universities, increasingly similar to the bloated state bureaucracies in form and spirit, create the same appeal. There is no evidence to support the claim that art in the Soviet Union flourishes as a result of the elevated social and economic status of artists. The artist needs more to be understood than to be fed, or drink Beefeater's gin, or enjoy a country club membership, or, for that matter, to have assorted fringe benefits.

So the artist comes into the community of professional scholars as a subsidized creature, like the research biologist or the social psychologist, but somehow plying a different trade from those worthy academics. He comes as either an ornament to an institution which can afford peripheral ornamentation, or as a journeyman-academic with a semisecret vice. What part is he to play within his employing institution beyond the discharge of his contracted-for services? The first problem to be confronted is the fact that his contributions are far more remote than those of any of his colleagues. His direct contributions to the local environs are nil, save for whatever public appearances he may feel disposed to make, and most of these would predictably be disasters. His participation within the life of the institution must necessarily be limited. He will be justifiably wary of much involvement in faculty affairs on the grounds that they are too time consuming and distracting, and he has relatively slight knowledge of the issues and problems involved; what ideas he might possess are likely to be exotic and disputatious. His fundamental work is really not research and cannot be so conceived. He does not contribute to further knowledge on the cure of hog cholera or the voting behavior of Jasper County. He may, in fact, even be an indifferent teacher within the conventional scope of the word. If he is a writer, even a Pulitzer Prize winner, he may be quite hopeless as a teacher of advanced composition. If he is a painter, he may not be able to vitally articulate his conceptions of his craft.

This does not sound like a description of an ideal faculty member. He doesn't bother with the Kiwanis Club, is not a valuable member of committees, doesn't appear to be advancing useful human knowledge, and may even, though not necessarily, be an indifferent general teacher. It might be even worse than this: heaven forbid, he might be an unruly type, nonconformist, argumentative, quarrelsome, or even given to flouting the regional moral strictures. What role can an individual like this play in the well-ordered routines of higher education?

He has two roles, I think, both vital and both substantially justifying his inclusion in the academic community, assuming for the moment that it is tenable for him to be so connected. First, the role of the artist in the academic community is identical with his role in the greater community, namely, to follow unequivocatingly the dictates of his own aesthetic sensitivities, to put into palpable form the fruits of his own peculiar talents, not alone to salve his own ego (although this is altogether necessary), but to provide his fellow men the continuity of beauty and subterranean understanding which has to date redeemed man from his jungle predispositions. Art cannot be other than a fragile, personal expression resting upon a ubiquitous human spirit, but a spirit which finds integration and realization within a limited segment of men.

Beyond this role, the artist-*cum*-academician has his own

institutionalized function as well. His effect on that priceless aspect of a university—its style or atmosphere—may be immense and in a quite personal way. After all, the artist's essential contact with life is rather different from the academic's; he views phenomena from different angles. In a very real sense, the artist is the more worldly of the two; he is far more involved with the significance and impact of much that would seem slight or inconsequential to those embarked on the pursuit of grander generalities, more comprehensive and coherent explanations. Also, the artist for all his usually brittle and reflective sophistication, also possesses a far more intense sensualism, much more akin to the sensual responses of the child. In large measure, this gives a perceptive artist a multidimensional view of the life that surrounds him and frequently imparts an engaging sense of proportion. This latter trait often takes the form of a high degree of sensitivity to the absurd, a condition not altogether unknown in collegiate communities. He becomes a useful counterirritant, a deflator of the inanely pretentious, the obtusely unworldly and, above all, the vulgar. Often the artist's influence is oblique, his participation in the style of his institution undefined and intermittent, but, I submit, of potentially incalculable value.

Further, the artist may contribute excitement, especially to the students, few or many, who seek him out and surround him. At base, this is the excitement that stems from being at close quarters with an individual in the heat of actual production. This contribution the artist shares with the working scholar, but there are many students whose dispositions are like his own, intoxicated with aesthetic nuance.

Thus, I believe the thesis can be defended that the artist *does* have a place, that advantages accrue to the academic communities which welcome him. But what of the advantages—and disadvantages—that may befall the artist in his dual role? The advantages are obvious—he has a clean, dry bed to sleep on (even if he has to exercise unusual discretion in whom he shares it with), food for himself and family, a not-too-onerous work routine (although this varies from institution to institution), a certain protective professional aloofness and, occasionally, a decent place to work. The question is, what price does he have to pay for it? He may not have had hot and cold running water in Montmartre, but there were few encumbrances. How much does one give up in moving from Greenwich Village or Big Sur to Swathmore or East Orange State? Is it a decent bargain?

I do not subscribe to the theory that the best art is produced in cold garrets. By and large, the best art is produced under reasonably comfortable conditions by reasonably well-adjusted human beings. Freezing studios and starvation diets do not stimulate art; they are rather handicaps that fail to get in the way of a serious artist. There is no reason why a mature artist cannot do admirable work under physically congenial circumstances. The trap of university life is that it might conceivably provide an environment too psychologically restful, with too many inducements to give up the craft in favor of talking about it. This is one of the prospective dangers, the built-in temptation for the artist to become a raconteur, a critic, an artistic gadfly, a hail fellow well met who plays at something he ought to take seriously.

Another threat comes from the opposite direction. In short, there are philistines entrenched in universities with the same sturdy resolve one meets with elsewhere. Often they have power and use it. The artist finds himself smothered; his creative instincts wither, stifled by the accumulated weight of the insensitivity, mediocrity, and middle-class self-approval; or his creative energies are provoked into senseless and ill-conceived rages, personal and creative. It is conceivable that universities can be wastelands, artistically and even intellectually, and that individual talents can be swallowed up, stilled by the numbing influence of organized philistinism. In society at large, more areas of retreat are available than in the semi-isolation of the university community. In the face of this situation, the artist might succumb or choose blatant rebellion. While there are notable exceptions, in general, art is not the result of this kind of localized insurgency.

I think, however, that a more subtle threat exists in the university to the creativity of the artist than these predominantly sociological factors. We might call this jeopardy "over-intellectualization," or the aesthetic trap of indulging in excessive intellectual or even overtly academic introspection and analysis. Let me make it clear that I am not advancing the cause of artistic primitivism. Quite the contrary, what I am asserting is that one's critical relationship with one's work is essentially in the area of craftsmanship and that it is markedly different from an intellectual appraisal. As an experiment, take a poem you have written and give it to students for analysis (author unidentified, of course) and you will discover all manner of fascinating intrepretations, many of them highly plausible and containing profounder implications than you ever dreamed of conveying—but you'll get precious little criticism of your prosody. This is a bad state of mind for the artist. He cannot be his own interpreter, author of his own *Key to Finnegans Wake*. Soon he will be hopelessly self-conscious. Alas, the intellectual communion has this potential effect upon the artist—he may be persuaded into taking himself seriously.

Too much intellectual exposure may also injure the purity of an artist's responses to experience, especially on a sensual level, although this is not invariably the case. I should think, however, a major in psychology would not be the happiest preparation for a novelist, or in architectural draftsmanship for a painter, or the most sanguine background for a composer, the advanced theories of the physics of sound. Above all, the artist must flee the professional jargonese, especially if words are to be his counters.

But we have not yet touched on what I think is the most

likely source of difficulty in the artist-academician consolidation. That is what I shall call the legitimate demand for artistic freedom. All of us are familiar with what is described as academic freedom. It is a very precious thing, a vital thing, a principle that involves the very substance of civilized continuity. I am all for it and for a quite broad interpretation of it. I believe, however, that the artist has some justification both for enjoying the benefits of the academic freedom that stems from his employment and for claiming an additional area of freedom from institutional and public infringement. It is this area which I have labeled "artistic freedom".

Academic freedom's prime value is that it provides for conditions of work under which academics can make their maximum contribution to society. But the artist's contribution is somewhat different; both his ends and means are different, and he requires different conditions of work. The most vital of all these conditions is the freedom of the artist to confront experience, in all its aspects, in any and all ways he deems rewarding to him as an artist. It is imperative that he do so, and he alone can be the judge of what types of confrontation are appropriate. As a free citizen, the artist has this opportunity in the sense that he can do as he chooses—and can also suffer whatever consequences may result. Surely if a writer decides to murder someone in order to discover the psychological impact of the act, he is also likely to become aware of what it feels like to sit in an electric chair. Artists have either conformed to or thumbed their noses at conventions since Homer.

We would be less than candid, however, if we were not to agree to the fact that joining a university faculty entails the imposition of certain restrictions, albeit gentle or subtle, that otherwise would not be imposed if a man were a bartender, a salesman, or even a lawyer. There still remains a certain clerical aura to the profession, and that has been reinforced by the lamentable "take care of our little girl" syndrome of

American higher education. However the profession of university teaching may wish otherwise; save perhaps at Bennington and the University of Chicago, academics are expected to adopt the mores of the middle-middle class. This may or may not be desirable, but in any case it does not seriously impair the work of the scholar, even that of the late professor of zoology at Indiana University.

Such implicit inhibitions are intolerable and unfair to the artist. The situation is made particularly acute by the popular misconception regarding morals. The word to the contemporary popular mind refers to only one thing: sexual promiscuity in various forms. This fixed idea has an intensely debilitating effect on the national morals in general, but it has put the stain of immorality across the practicing artist in all media, since all media are concerned with reflecting at least in part our contemporary milieu, and in this post-Freudian era the phallic image seems inexorable.

Let us take a hypothetical example. I am willing to defend the premise that Vladimir Nabokov is a writer of the first rank and that *Lolita* is a novel of unusual artistic merit. Let us not even bother with the question of whether Nabokov would have continued his academic employment if he had been an unknown novelist and had published *Lolita* as a first effort. The answer would, I assume, depend on the institution. There is a deeper question. Suppose Nabokov had spent the bulk of his adult life as a college professor. Could he have written *Lolita?* Could he have acquired the insights, the nuances, the sense of human variety, within the confines of an American university or college? The answer must be random speculation, but I am tempted to guess. The point to be made is that if the university is to become a wholesome sanctuary for the artist, it must be willing to permit a freedom of personal experiment and involvement on the part of the artist that hitherto has existed only in exceptional institutions.

I think this is a thorny problem—a Gordian knot. The

issue of artistic freedom on the campus involves personal conduct because that is a part of the artist's basic equipment. And contemporary American art is not all Edna Ferber, Edna St. Vincent Millay, Grant Wood, or Norman Rockwell. Our times would be most inadequately chronicled by these alone.

If the artist is to do more than illuminate old manuscripts or write graduation odes in his new bailiwick, the limits of his freedom may need redefining, and artistic freedom wedded to academic freedom. This is undeniably a difficult symbiosis to conceive. It runs counter to the prevailing mood of much of American higher education, since it appears ready to embrace a philosophy of mass instruction and social relativism. To the extent that colleges and universities become popular institutions, in the generic sense, they become increasingly sensitive to popular prejudices and pressures. The university in becoming a so-called "service institution" begins the gradual and irrevocable process of broadening the concept of community service until it becomes defined as any and all demands made upon the educational community by the public at large. It is dubious, to say the least, that such a process would be conducive to the freedom of intellectual inquiry in general and, especially and in particular, to an expanded concept of the personal freedom of the publicly subsidized artist.

The startling expansion of higher education in terms of its availability and the accompanying diversity of the educational product has already placed considerable strain upon the instructional resources of many universities. Staffing worries, now only mildly troublesome, are likely to become critical in the next decade. It may become a matter in some areas and in some institutions of merely finding faculty to man the multiplying classrooms. This problem of educational logistics does not bode well for the encouragement of artistic endeavors on the campus. There will be an unmistakable temptation to dragoon working artists into instructional loads wholly incompatible with continued artistic production.

In another sense, the teaching responsibilities of university employment present further ramifications quite beyond the issue of the allocation of time. I refer to the psychological reconciliation of pedagogy and creativity. It need not at all be the case that the act of teaching is in some fashion depressing to the artistic imagination as is sometimes supposed. The artist, quite like the academic, can use the instructional phase as a useful experience, often permitting a handy testing area for ideas or as a means of gauging the prevailing mood. Turned the other way around, the work of the artist, again similar to that of the scholar, is a tremendously vivifying influence on the practice of teaching. It seems astonishing that even yet the notion persists that teaching and scholarship or creativity are basically unrelated and even hostile enterprises. One can hear even today references to "teaching institutions" and "research institutions," or remarks dividing "teachers" and "scholars." This would appear to be a most artificial division, if for no other reason than that it is hard to envision any stimulating university instruction that is not the reasonably connected by-product of the instructor's continued personal interests and growth in his selected field. Only on the basis of persistent personal intellectual cultivation can truly effective teaching rest.

The same values accrue from the work of the artist-academician, not only in his direct specialized confrontations, but also less directly in the qualities of mind the artist can bring to teaching. The artist is a curious blend of usually unassailable self-confidence, even egoism, with a parallel sense of humility in the face of his creative undertakings, and an acute awareness of the enormity of the challenge. In most instances, he approaches his pedagogical duties in this same frame of mind. These attitudes, almost instantaneously cognizable by students, have an immensely salutary effect on undergraduate reactions to intellectual work. The artist's pervading confidence in his ability to cope ultimately with his artistic difficulties can act as a tonic on undergraduate diffidence. The artist's sense of humility, his almost instinctive awareness of the cruel demands of standards, and, above all else, his recognition of human fallibility (his realization of human-ness), cut like a sharp blade through the regrettable mysticism of university pedagogy, its occasional stuffiness, pomposity, austerity, and tendency toward uncritical conventionalism. It would be difficult to gauge the possible effects upon a student of drinking a few beers with Karl Shapiro or taking a walk in the woods with Walter Van Tilburg Clark. What is the hidden touchstone of the process that provokes the human spirit into seeking higher ground? Whom would we choose to sit on the other end of the log?

Or put it another way. In Plato's celebrated allegory of the Cave in *The Republic,* the process of human enlightenment is couched in somewhat curious language, in that those who find truth, those who escape from the darkness of the Cave, are described as being "dragged" up the heights and "compelled" to look at the light. They who do the dragging and the compelling are not identified by Plato. Who are they? I leave the question with you to ponder.

Finally, when we pull all the threads of our reflections together, we are faced with the one stubborn question: Does the academic community and the general public really wish to support art on art's own terms? I think you will agree that the stickler in the question is the matter of "art's own terms." Certainly there can be no real doubt that the general public and the academic community would agree to support art on *their* terms. No society, primitive or civilized, has been totally without some form of aesthetic expression and production. It is equally true that the quality of art present in these societies, diverse time and locale, is largely a matter of whether that art was an expression of creative will or whether it was principally a decorative expression of mass sentiment, in other words, art in the direct service of social institutions.

The most formidable obstacle to the propagation of art both in society and the academic world is that neither of these social divisions believes that art (and by implication, the artist) can be trusted to its own will, its own devices. This is not because the belief in the demonic character of art endures, but rather that art socially undirected is likely to become trivial, even infantile, and, above all, irresponsible. One suspects that this conception is largely the product of a lingering romanticism in the public's view—notions about art as the flowering of unworldly and undisciplined minds, art as unbridled and even sophomoric subjectivism, art as being a form of social revolt, even anti-intellectual agitation. All these half-articulated popular assumptions are made, of course, in the face of the fact that contemporary art is the virtual antithesis of these characteristics. The end result is a sort of social paternalism in regard to art, metaphorically, the relationship of a middle-aged father to a colorful but unstable child.

The artist, wherever he is, on a campus or on a Connecticut farm, lives out his creative life under this quite galling interdict, this veiled suggestion that he must endure some gentle form of social guidance for his own good. The astonishing thing is that he continues to work, continues to make his contribution to the commonweal. He does it under the misconceived but benevolent auspices of American society, but he did it, too, under medieval despots, Renaissance autocrats, even under the more terrifying repressions of the twentieth-century Attilas. The reason he does it is because, in the last hard analysis, he serves himself—not the state, not the community, not the people, and not the university. His is a private passion.

VII

THE
TWENTIETH CENTURY MIND

WE CAN ALL begin with one common denominator: we are all, for good or ill and without the exercise of choice, inhabitants of the planet during an era designated by our conventional Western calendar as the twentieth century. Opinions vary as to whether this particular temporal residence is a fortuitous accident. Much has been made of glorious human advancements that have marked this century, the technological wonders, the humanitarian boons, the growing conquest of the environment. It has been described as an exciting, if unsettling, period in which to live. It is, of course, the century of nuclear discovery and utilization; it is the century of space exploration. It is a time of "new frontiers," "great societies," promises of worldwide affluence, the final vanquishing of many of man's most stubborn enemies: poverty, disease, ignorance, and even war. It is a time of the ascendency of human capability.

Not all estimations of the collective mind of the era are as sanguine or as complimentary. Cecil Rhodes, in a hiatus of national vanity, once remarked that "being born an Englishman was like winning first prize in a lottery." Some observers have conversely contended that being thrust into the twentieth century was not exactly like grabbing the cultural brass ring and, indeed, that this period of human history was one more likely to induce a sense of shame than one of prideful accomplishment. The philosopher Eliseo Vivas has commented that "it is one of the marks of human decency to be ashamed of having been born into the twentieth century."

It is not an altogether perverse evaluation. Surely accuracy would require that this century be also designated as a segment of the human narrative notable for unequaled mass

119

savagery, wholly unrivaled destruction, and the creation of the power, perhaps even the will, to destroy the totality of civilized life. On subtler grounds, it might be argued too that although our times have produced spectacular material productivity, ours is an epoch of mass unrest and dissatisfaction, societal dislocation, whether of spiritual, cultural, or psychological origin. Is man either happier or better (in some admittedly vague moralistic sense) in 1966 than he was in 1766 or even 1266? It is an intriguing question and gives rise to the fascinating, if frustrating, game of comparing on some adumbrated scale of values the relative worth of centuries— a sort of dialectical tampering about with the idea of progress.

This motif of progress underlies these differing attitudes toward the twentieth century. Few if any today embrace a complete comprehensive meliorism, the doctrine of the inevitability of progress. But the melioristic momentum of the nineteenth century is still with us, especially in the United States, perhaps the last major power to emerge from the influences of this past era and even now in part nostalgically hankering after its reassuring simplicities. However, the antimelioristic reaction is well marked, culminating in a sort of contemporary pessimism notable in a number of current philosophical and ideological movements. The truth is that we are well past the mid-point of the century without any serious attention to what in the last century was called the "philosophy of history" and this omission renders systematic evaluation difficult. Obviously any judgment of the twentieth century rests on some variety of supposition as to the nature of the historical process: forthright meliorism, cyclic conceptions, dialectical views, history as *geistewissenshaften,* and so on.

Judgment, then, may have to be suspended if only for the reason that it would imply all manner of philosophic biases. In lieu of an agreed historical scale of values or even a consensus as to the nature of history, we are forced to fall back on analysis, a specie of the restoration or recreative theory of history. But however appealing may be this orientation, so persuasively espoused in this century by Collingwood and Croce, among others, the bleak question is whether we can analyze our time while still being participants in it? Here again, the matter of judgment may elude us, on historical as well as philosophic grounds, but interpretation and clarification appear to be demanded of us, a sort of inescapable mandate, a vital prerequisite to the salvation of sanity in the here and now.

The term "mind" is admittedly an illusive one, a short noun useful in constructing lecture titles, but in need of substantial clarification before we proceed to analyze the intellectual drift of the twentieth century. The word "mind" can designate, of course, that particular human faculty identified with the processes of thought. In this context, it is a term not as popular in this century as the last, but it can be employed to identify the area concerned with the examination of thought in a restrictive, psychobiological sense. Certainly the strides recently taken in the area of cybernetics and the study of brain circuitry and its attendant impact on current epistemology is a classification that will later merit our attention.

Beyond this, the appellation "mind" has been used two ways in our contemporary lexicon. In one sense, it designates the nature of what might be called sophisticated or esoteric intellectual reflection—the character of philosophic speculation, the more articulate forms of ideology or systematic social criticism.

In another aspect, mind might refer to mass consciousness, impelling motivations for popular convictions and movements, the *folkgeist,* the subterranean rationale for mass behavior, social emergences, political dogma. Clearly both forms of the word are legitimate and both must be the object of analysis, but in attempting to weigh their proportionate significances, their interrelationship may prove provocative.

It can be argued with considerable persuasiveness that a genetic link exists, that popular opinions, tastes, movements do not arise *sui generis,* but must have a causation, however transmitted, and that the popular ethos is the result of the transmigration of more abstract and theoretical thought. The "popular mind," put in other language, is the result of the filtering down of ideas from the rarified air of self-conscious philosophy to the level of social usage. This is quite frankly a mysterious process (and one relatively unexplored by intellectual historians) and it involves not only tracing the skein of inheritance, but, also, systematically describing the time-lag factor implied. Some convincing evidence can be brought forth to indicate that patterns exist in the gap in time between the arising of an idea or concept in the area of what might be called "professional" philosophy and its reappearance as a segment of popular doctrine. This downward vector in the movement of ideas, crossing a hierarchically organized social structure, has applications in the areas of symbol and art as well.

But an equally intelligible contention would be that the lower intellectual strata, lower both in the ontological and social sense, produce the higher; philosophy, art, and even science result from the bubbling up to the articulate surface from the mass consciousness, a view advanced by Marx, Bergson, and Tolstoy, among others, in various forms and connections. This point of view, while intriguing, rests on quite as enigmatic relationships as does its opposite theory.

In the main, however, the case appears stronger for those who advocate the downward assimilation theory, and we might be prudent to proceed on our exploration by first examining some pertinent aspects of theoretic speculation and then move on to consider the flux of popular ideas, passions, and mores.

There is one more reservation to be made, that is, it is quite obviously impossible to offer an omnibus account of the history of ideas in our century. Time-space imposes selectivity. The basis of that selectivity must be those ideas whose impact upon our times appears most likely to be both lasting and truly formative, indeed, those subterranean convolutions that determine the courses of human affairs and crucially espoused values.

Combining, then, both the philosophic and ideologic factors in our analysis of the character of the twentieth-century mind, perhaps it is possible to systematize our observations under five rather broad headings:

1. The Rediscovery of the Trans-personal Content of Mind
2. The Fall of Mechanism and Reductionism in Science
3. The Trauma of Spiritual Alienation
4. The Redefinition of Social Freedom
5. The Era of Anti-Politics

The Rediscovery
of the Trans-personal Content of Mind

The focal problem of our century centers about attempts to understand human behavior—to frame a tenable and synthetic philosophy of human nature. No one can fail to be impressed by the volume and range of empirical investigation of man in all his various aspects. The regrettable feature of this exploration, however, is its fragmentization, its mass of unrelated and unintegrated data. No core concept of man emerges, no generally agreed-upon formulation of the first-order premises; indeed, there is even little intelligible communication between the legions of human researchers. Psychologists often cannot converse with anthropologists, social philosophers and biologists operate with separate conceptual frames, and even the professional vocabularies are mutually exclusive. The simplicities and consensus that marked philosophies of human nature from Scholasticism to the mid-nineteenth century have vanished, chased away by the imperative authority of a broadening science of man.

Yet no alternative synthesis, no reformulation, arose to replace the at least useful classical definitions of human nature. The result has been a sort of theoretic paralysis in which both speculative and normative axiological philosophy has lain dormant in our century. There is an obvious dearth of speculative theorizing in political philosophy, historical scholarship falls prey to positivism, and a rift widens between moral and empirical reflections on human behavior. Even the most practical and yet awesome problems of political arrangement—war and peace, international concord—are stymied for want of a new synthesis that will put man back together in an organic sense, and will provide a rigorous base on which to rest more explicit comprehensive social thought. This is the great frontier of the twentieth century—the mind itself.

One of the major stumbling blocks to a new synthesis of knowledge about man stems from the persistence in various forms of a concept of mind lingering from the Enlightenment in general and John Locke in particular. In brief, it is the concept of the human mind as, in Locke's borrowed phrase (from Aquinas), a *tabula rasa,* an empty slate upon which experience writes. Man is thought of as entering upon life as a neutral blob of sense perception, subsequently molded by the enounter with his external world. Of course, this is a brutally terse presentation of the idea, but it is just to say that this subjectivism in various subtler forms continues to permeate contemporary thought, from psychological environmentalism to cultural relativism.

This view of man has one crucial operational defect: it fails to provide an adequate explanation of phenomena, either in individual or cultural terms. Environmental influences, however well scrutinized, do not account for considerable areas of both human mental activity and cultural data. But although the twentieth century began with a general dedication to the fragmentary and reductionistic theories of human nature influenced by Enlightenment epistemology, as the century progresses there are striking shifts of viewpoint. These are sufficiently numerous to suggest a most provocative possibility—that we will see in our era that needed integration of concepts of human nature, a new synthesis, a new general theory of man. This may well be both the most important intellectual current of our times and the most exciting and promising aspect of our quest for understanding. There are substantial evidences of a melding of human knowledge, a cross-fertilization of our heretofore isolated investigations. The potentialities of such a concresence are immense and may affect the historical drift of the remainder of the epicycle.

To be more specific, the prospects for a comprehensive philosophy of human nature appear to be rooted in an expanding interrelationship between four major areas of thought: dynamic psychology; neurology and neuro-biology, with emphasis on cybernetic research; meta-anthropology; realist theories of ontology.

The result of this fusion of knowledge is leading us to a rejection of *tabula rasa* theories of mind and environmental reductionism and cultural relativism. Put another way: a definition of human nature must involve the identification and recognition of elements beyond those provided by an exclusively empirical examination of phenomena—man is something more than his experience. How can this hypothesis be asserted?

Beginning with Freud and continuing with Jung and analytical psychology, the premise clearly emerges that human behavior, indeed, human personality, contains decisive elements that are extraexperiential. In dynamic psychology there is a multitude of well-known illustrations of this premise: "racial memory," the "collective unconscious," the *"participation mystique,"* the theory of the archetype, and so on. The key here is the role of symbol in its universal role as converter or, as Joseph Campbell nicely puts it, the "inherited image." The problem is to rationally confront the implications posed by the ubiquity of symbolism—the question of "innate ideas," the question of "psychic inheritance," even another look at the question of "instinct."

It is at this point where contemporary neurological research is especially fascinating in its attempts to explain these extraexperiential phases of mental life. We might take three examples: the theory of the "innate releasing mechanism"; the McCulloch-Pitt experiments with "trapped universals"; the demonstration by the late Norbert Wiener and others that the human nervous system is a teleological mechanism.

The term "innate releasing mechanism"—or IRM—is employed by biologists to describe that factor in the nervous systems of animals that appears to have its genesis in inherited structure, allowing the animal to react to situations previously entirely unknown to the organism. Newly-hatched chickens, for example, flee in terror from the sight of a hawk or even a model of that bird of prey, but remain entirely tranquil when exposed to ducks or pigeons.[1] This factor, IRM, is manifestly transpersonal, to use the Jungian terminology. In the human situation, the IRM may correspond to the concept of the archetype or "primary image" which Jung identifies as a "memory deposit, an engram, derived from a condensation of innumerable similar experiences . . . the psychic expression of an anatomically, physiologically determined natural tendency."[2] The findings of animal and human psychology are obviously related to the extent that the central nervous systems of animals demonstrate the existence of innate structure or content related to the functioning environment. The animal facing his environment copes with it by immediate direction and recognition,

1   The illustration is supplied by Joseph Campbell in his general discussion of IRM in Chapter 1, in *Primitive Mythology: The Masks of God* (Viking Press: New York, 1959.) I am indebted to Campbell's discussion of IRM and have incorporated portions of it in my description.

2   *Ibid.*, 32.

not through the ponderous process of environmental experience. These structures or contents are variously designated —the Gestalt term "isomorph" is a useful label.

This isomorphic structure by no means exhausts the potentialities of mind, since the process of adaption as well involves individual variation and learning—the IRM is susceptible to the imprint of learning. But we are growingly aware of the fact that the human animal, possessing innate releasing mechanisms, is highly sensitive to a series of "sign stimuli" or, in neurological language, "central excitatory mechanisms." But the instinctual mechanism in man is far more "open" than in the lower animals; moreover, some biologists have been intrigued by the possibility that man has been affected by a series of inhibiting mutations. Further it has been suggested that these physiological shortcomings have provoked compensations, have provided man with an amazingly intricate and variegated spectrum of sign stimuli, the range of his emotions and creativity. But such human variation and novelty apparently arise from a foundation of innate mechanism.

Some recent speculation has been that IRM can be triggered by sign stimuli *not* a feature of the natural environment and that the IRM mechanisms when so stimulated are even more intense. Religion, myth, and ritual have been cited as being in this class of supernormal sign stimuli. Such suppositions are quite evidently hypothetical, but there is every reason to assume that we are only on the threshold of discovery regarding the relationship between culturally conditioned and instinctual behavior. The problem of the priority of instinctual or innate patterns remains a dilemma even in the less complicated animals, to say nothing of the correspondence, neurological and psychological, of man and animals. But the riddle of mechanism may be capable of solution.

We can now turn to the neurological experiments of Mc-Culloch and Pitt and the Rosenblueth-Wiener-Bigelow theory of teleological mechanism. A full description of the technical theory developed by McCulloch and Pitt is beyond our purposes here, but the pertinent elements of it can be sketched. McCulloch, a neurologist, and Pitt, a symbolic logician, became convinced that an "epistemic rule of correspondence exists between the introspected primitive ideas and postulates of symbolic logic" and the "logical relatedness of nerve cells and events in the human system and especially in the cortex." Or, put another way: there are "neural physiological public epistemic correlates of a privately introspected and remembered idea."[3] This proposition appeared tenable on the basis of the discovery that nerve cells in cortical neural nets are ordered in circles as well as in lineal order. If only the latter form of neural nets existed, it would be evident that no nervous system—human or machine—could possibly retain introduced data conveyed by the sensory neurons. In short, the introspected fact of "memory" would be dubious, except in a vague epiphenomenal sense. In circular neural nets, however, retention is possible, the neural net being able to restore its potential energy while at the same time preserving the imprint of the original ideational data. These neural nets represent an ordered sequence of the "firing" of nerve cells. These "firings" or "explosions" feature a measurable gap of time (termed a "synapse"). This concept of "synaptic time" is important in grasping the idea that the circular neural net is constantly in the process of self-restoration before the completion of the circuit. The firing of the concluding neurons of the net reactivates the restored neurons of the initial phases of the circuit, assuming a constant metabolic process, for

3   F. S. C. Northrop, *Philosophical Anthropology and Practical Politics* (Macmillan: New York, 1960), 48. His chapter "The Neurological Epistemic Correlates of Introspected Ideas" is an invaluable source, and I acknowledge my reliance on it. See also Chapter 10, F. S. C. Northrop, *The Logic of the Sciences and Humanities* (Macmillan: New York, 1947), and F. S. C. Northrop, *Cybernetics*, ed. Heinz von Foerster (Josiah Macy, Jr., Foundation: New York, 1949–53).

even as long as the life of the organism. Thus the impulse cannot escape from the circuit, constituting what McCulloch calls a "trapped univeral" or "reverberating circuit," and it becomes, within the nervous system, the epistemic correlate of directly introspected ideas, although not the introspected memory of a specific idea of meaning. The trapped universal is the mechanism of primary recognition or general instinctual pattern. Some experimental neurologists contend that even the lower animals possess representations of earlier stimuli beyond the reverberating circuits. When McCulloch and Pitt probed deeper into the nature of the trapped impulse, another characteristic was revealed. Not only was a trapped impulse a persisting causal representation of a past event, but it was also a symbolic reconstitution of that event, in short, a symbol, an abstraction. Moreover, a trapped figure of circulating impulses can have the formal property of representing a class of similar particulars or, in other words, the trapped impulse becomes a formal concept or, finally, what McCulloch wishes to call a "trapped universal." The neurological-psychological ramifications of this concept are far-reaching, but perhaps the most formidable is the assertion of mechanical causation. How can this mechanism be made compatible with the idea of purposeful and self-directed human behavior? One reasonable response would be that trapped impulses of emotion, aesthetic experience, or complex images are as readily fixed as more prosaic epistemic images of trees, rocks, or billboards.

But perhaps the more significant answer is that the mechanism reveals an innate teleological structure. This is a bold claim in the face of the contention of much of current mathematical physics that physical systems alter their conditions mechanically rather than teleologically. Nonetheless, Norbert Wiener offered the rebuttal to this widely held view by arguing that there exist teleological mechanical systems characterized by a self-governing negative "feedback" which he chose to call "cybernetics" (from the Greek root meaning "helmsman," by the way). F. S. C. Northrop has compared Wiener's concept of feedback in the human nervous system to the operation of an antiaircraft gun:

An antiaircraft gun (1) fires a projectile at an airplane, (2) has within itself an apparatus which receives electromagnetic waves from its own moving projectile and from the continuously moving airplane and (3) mechanically self-corrects the direction in which the next projectile is fired if the data of (2) indicate that the previously fired projectile is missing its target. When, on the other hand, no miss is occurring, the old motor response is reinforced and the feedback is positive. The notable characteristic of such a mechanism is that it mechanically self-directs and corrects its own motor responses with respect to stimuli received from some target and from the machine's projected response to that target in such a way that any discrepancy between the projected motor response and the target mechanically causes the present or later response to hit the target. In short, by means of mechanical causality alone a miss mechanically necessitates a later hit.

It is to be noted also that in any negative feedback mechanism, the final state of the entire system is a mechanically causal function of both the target or goal and the intervening states of the motor response of the system. Since teleological behavior is behavior in which the final state is a function not merely of the initial stage of the system but also of its later future states, such a mechanical system behaves teleologically and is, therefore, appropriately called a teleological mechanism.[4]

If one combines the McCulloch-Pitt investigations with this cybernetic feedback there emerges an intriguing possibility. Is there any reason the feedback target in the nervous

4   Northrop, *Philosophical Anthropology and Practical Politics*, 68. See also, A. Rosenblueth, N. Wiener, J. Bigelow, "Behavior, Purpose and Teleology," *Journal of the Philosophy of Science*, X (1943), 18–24; N. Wiener, *Cybernetics* (Wiley: New York, 1948), and N. Wiener, *The Human Use of Human Beings* (Doubleday: New York, 1954).

system cannot be the trapped impulses that are the correlates of an individual's fundamental concepts, indeed, his
very philosophic underpinnings? Are we not closer to an
adequate description of the "isomorph," the mechanics of
the innate releasing mechanism? Here lie the explanations
for the universality of cortical activity, an empirically
verifiable account of sign stimuli and symbol and, incidentally, the prospects for the construction of high-level com-
puters capable of reproducing an extraordinary range of
human accomplishments.

There are broader reasons, however, for our brief sortie
into the area of neurological research. As one can perceive,
there is a clustering of concepts between depth psychology
and neurobiology which cogently imply a multidimensional
view of mind, a conception of mind that posits two fundamental propositions: (1) Human nature contains crucial extraexperiential, transpersonal content, and psychic inheritance looms as a major factor in behavior; (2) Individual
human behavior and culture rest on the existence of universals, present as innate structure in the personality, as
archetypal sign stimuli, both natural and supernormal and
present as cultural artifact.

We have been dealing with these synthesizing propositions as they affect the individual organism, but they are also
inferential in the wider scope of social and cosmic organism.
In the latter case, there are significant correlations between
ontological theory and the nature of man. This realization
takes us quite logically into the burgeoning area of meta-
anthropology and the new ontologies of which Alfred North
Whitehead's pan-psychist "philosophy of organism" will
serve as an admirable example.

The tenor of the meta-anthropology to which we have
referred is well observed in the *Eranos* Yearbooks, published
continuously since 1933. These annual publications record
meetings held in Switzerland devoted to the discussion of

depth analysis of transcultural phenomena. The term *eranos*, incidentally, was selected by the Marburg philosopher, Rudolph Otto, and means a meal to which each makes his contribution. The connection between the *Eranos* gatherings and German philosophic neorealism is by no means accidental. In the main this new anthropology is strongly influenced by Freudian and Jungian psychology and such contemporary philosophic realists as Otto, N. Hartmann, and Max Scheler. Names that might be mentioned in the movement include Erich Neumann, Hans Leisegang, C. Kerenyi, Géza Roheim, and Mircea Eliade.

At base, this meta-anthropology is an avowal of cultural universalism, the analysis of mythology as archetypal projection, and the integration of theories of culture with both psychological dynamism and ontological realism. Nicolai Hartmann has succinctly presented the vital orientations of this anthropology:

The older theories of the spirit all shied away from incorporating non-spiritual factors into the structure of the spiritual world. They feared thereby to fall prey to materialism. But there is no cause for this apprehension, provided the mistake is not made of setting up a radical either-or, as if by admitting certain organic components everything in the realm of the spirit becomes at once dependent on the organism. Non-spiritual factors of highly divergent types may very well enter without the spiritual life losing its uniqueness and characteristic independence. For all spirit rests on the broader cosmic context and depends on it. It must, therefore, include, and be subject to, the manifold threads of determination, not created by it, which form the cosmic context. But that does not prevent it from having its own self-determination and from confronting the powers of lower nature with a very definite independence.

The new anthropology rediscovers these relationships. It has room for the autonomy of spiritual life, but knows, also, how to unite with it the organic stratum of the human being. That is possible only on the basis of certain ontological ideas. The absolute self-sufficiency of the spirit as defended by idealist theories cannot then be maintained. But the autonomy of the spirit does not depend on doctrines of this type which are at variance with the phenomena. All independence of the spirit which we know is independence is dependence, and the dependence is a weighty and many-sided one. To dispute this dependence would be closing one's eyes to the facts. But a reconciliation of dependence with independence can be accomplished only by an ontological clarification of the basic relationship between the heterogenous strata of reality.[5]

Thus far we are able to *reject* two prevailing assumptions: (1) human atomism—or as the American anthropologist Ralph Linton once put that thesis: "A society is a group of biologically distinct and self-contained individuals"; and (2) cultural relativism or the contention that cultural development contains no superorganic cross cultural or universal elements, and that separate cultures exist *causa sui*.

Speculative philosophy reinforces our schema for a new synthesis, but not unanimously by any means. The most direct support comes from such pan-psychist realists as Whitehead and Alexander; realist ontologists and moralists such as Hartmann and Scheler; the impressive phalanx of logical realism, assorted historically oriented metaphysicians as Croce and Collingwood; and substantial elements of contemporary phenomenology, especially Husserl. This is a formidable array, but it must be balanced against the influences of the various forms of positivism and certain elements of what has been rather loosely labeled as "existentialism."

Whitehead's impressive metaphysical edifice offers perhaps the most intimate correlation. No attempt can be made here to even offer a thumbnail account of the philosophy of organism, but a few selected aspects of Whitehead's metaphysics may illustrate how it provides a first-order catego-

5 Nicolai Hartmann, *New Ways of Ontology*, trans. Reinhard C. Kuhn (Regnery: Chicago, 1952), 41–42.

rial scheme for the synthesis. First, there is the concept that reality is not identified with substance, but may be defined as interrelatedness—that these rules of relationship are not static or mechanical, but dynamic and teleological—that, indeed, reality must be defined in terms of "process." This interrelatedness involves both the macrocosm and the microcosm, depicting nature in terms of nets of "actual occasions" projected through the mechanism of psychic inheritance. Whitehead attempts to dispel what he feels is the major ontological fallacy, what he dubs the "bifurcation of nature," the fallacy of static atomism. A feature of this incredibly dense interrelatedness is the prevalence of universals—Whitehead terms them "eternal objects"—manifest as factors in the concrescence of actual occasions, from the bipolarity of atomic particles to the integrations of conscious ideation. Additionally, he provides the concept of "prehension" or "feeling," maintaining that the fabric of this interrelatedness lies in varying strata of recognition and response, the great bulk of which remains below the level of consciousness and even sense data in the conventional sense. It is without equivocation the ontological and epistemological correlate of our more particularized biological and neurological concepts.

Thus philosophy, anthropology, neurology, biology, and psychology move in our century toward a new vision of man, a depiction more reconciling man and nature, explaining and stressing the continuity of process and the fact that man is an inheritor, not an isolated traveler on the continuum of cosmic experience and cultural metamorphosis. The "wholeness" of man and his rationale rather than vanity-inspired uniqueness in the conflux of nature may be the gift of the twentieth century and its thought. Such a contribution may, in the longer view of the epoch, be more far-reaching for human good than the willful harnessing of our physical environment.

The Fall of Mechanism and Reduction in Science

The twentieth century has seen a revolution in science, not solely in its obvious accomplishments that have so altered the nature of human life, but a revolution involving the *weltanschauung* of science itself, its base orientations and its methodology. The close of the nineteenth century saw the very foundations of science being rent by rational demolitions. Two of the most striking examples were the demise of mechanistic theories of physical laws and the threatening proposition that hitherto conventional mathematics contained irremediable flaws—in short, the fall of Newtonian physics and Euclidian geometry.

The revolution was even more profound than this, since it represented the virtual collapse of the classical rationalism in the philosophy of science that claimed more or less uninterrupted sway since the Aristotelian doctrine of essential nature. The assault on the citadel of scientific rationalism was intense. Newtonian mechanics gave way before the impact of quantum theory, its more unsettling aspect being illustrated by the Copenhagen school in general and Heisenberg's Principle of Indeterminacy in particular. It was appalling to those accustomed to the ordered confidences of Newtonian physics to be informed that the energy emission of atoms was unaccountably irregular. The cosmological implications were pregnant and disturbing. This disturbance was felt no less in mathematics where Euclidian geometry and conventional algebraic constructs were riddled by the analysis of nineteenth century mathematicians.

Following this demolishment at least two conclusions were evident. First, it was a fallacious oversimplification to assume that there did not exist virtually unlimited available schematic devices for ordering nature and that any claim to evidence based exclusively upon one was untenable. Second, it was evident that science proceeds on some conventional bases that are not necessarily rooted in either rational or empirical considerations, yet these conventions play a significant role in both the interpretation of data and the creation of theory. It was equally clear that these conventions represented philosophic dispositions and involvements more critical to scientific investigation than had hitherto been imagined. The fault, if it can be so termed, lay not solely with the philosophic naivete of practicing scientists, but with the failure of students of metaphysics to function in their appropriate role—as Collingwood puts it, in what he calls his "metaphysical rubric": ". . . in such and such phase of scientific thought it is (or was) absolutely presupposed that. . . ."

A core difficulty in this collapse of hallowed scientific postulates was the prevalence of the "correspondence theory of truth" in scientific investigation, and science's failure to abandon this specific and dubious orientation in favor of conceptions of truth as "coherence." Milton Munitz rather neatly sums this up by commenting:

Theories are apt or fitting but they are not as such *true,* where truth is taken to mean "correspondence" of symbol and existence. Indeed, to speak of fittingness can itself be a misleading analogy. In the case of a suit that is made to fit a man, we can measure and describe the body of a man *independently* of the suit. But in the case of theories, as in the case of languages, it is meaningless to think of nature as possessing its own code which might in principle be explored independently of our symbolism and a test carried out to see which one of our human devices most accurately "matches" the "real" one. Taking seriously the symbolic and constructive character of the theories of science means reorienting our conception of truth as a goal for science. It means giving up the "spectator" conception of knowledge and the "one-shot" criterion of adequacy.[6]

6 Milton Munitz, *Space, Time and Creation* (Collier Books: New York, 1957), 57–58.

Twentieth century science began a major reconstruction. Whitehead and Russell provided mathematics with a new legitimacy in their *Principia Mathematica,* employing symbolic logic as a restorative base. Poincaré, Gauss, Rieman, Lobachevsky reworked geometry. Einstein, Planck, Bohr, Eddington, Lemaitre, Milne, and others pushed on with logically oriented physics.

The new science could be characterized in four ways: (1) a new recognition of the limitations of induction and the certainty to be accorded empirical observation; (2) a revised estimate of both the diversity of the universe and its possible instability and lack of causal regularity; (3) an abandonment of the Aristotelian subject-object bifurcation as a methodological given; (4) a growing reliance on a coherence concept of theoretical truth.

Science's candid and searching recognition of its problems should (but it does so only rarely) point an example to those other areas of human investigation that currently yearn so intensely for the elegancies of pure science. A new social science, for example, if it ever comes, cannot avoid a corresponding transmutation.

THE TRAUMA OF SPIRITUAL ALIENATION

After the sturdy optimisms of the nineteenth century (Tennyson's "Better fifty years of Europe than a cycle of Cathay") our times have produced a deep uneasiness, an anxiety not totally explainable by the frightening aspect of nuclear weaponry. A kind of confused and even desperate introspection has overcome the mind of the West. It is perhaps more than the psychic dislocations of a culture undergoing a too rapid change under the hammerings of technological invention, industrialization, urbanization, and the attendant sociological consequences. The stark fact that more hospital beds in the United States are occupied by mental patients than by those put there by other forms of illness is a sobering piece of data and, indeed, does point to a number of social challenges. But in an even wider sense, it might be suggested that beyond the vast numbers of persons suffering from specific emotional action there exists an almost universal trauma, a profound sense of emptiness, a subterranean fear, a spiritual malady, if you will. It is the twentieth century disease.

It has been variously diagnosed—from Jung to Billy Graham. Look at any shelf of current books. The titles stare out at you—*Modern Man in Search of His Soul, The Sane Society, The Age of Anxiety, Life Against Death* and so on, to that proliferation of psychological "self-help" essays designed to teach you how to get along with your tensions and frustrations. Even LSD and other hallucinatory drugs have been submitted as a possible solution to this contemporary disorder of the spirit. This is neither surprising nor novel since "lotus-eating" as a means of solving painful dilemmas has had its advocates from the sojourners in Epicurus' garden, through generations of ascetics and mystics, to our current pseudophilosophies of personal noninvolvement. Retreat or the suspension of the critical faculties was a much more tenable alternative in past epochs anyway—in our century even Shangri-La was literally invaded by armies and politicians.

One of the wisest men of the last century, Friederich Nietzsche, made the oft-quoted observation that "God is dead, Man has slain him." The twentieth century reveals this as a substantial truth, both on grounds of metaphysical advocacy and as a psychoanthropological phenomenon. Man has indeed slain God as a rational fact of his cosmology and as a projection of his psychic need. The result is crucial. Whether such a demolition of the idea of God as either a cosmic or as a psychological rationale is philosophically justifiable or socially desirable is an open question; it is worthy, at least, of dialectical treatment. But our purpose is to explore the ramifications of one inescapable conclusion: Christianity in the West has ceased to be a vital or central ingredient in our emerging society. Eschewing the debate over whether or not this is in the long run a boon or a calamity, the collapse of Christianity was and is inevitable within the climate of our era. The primary problem is to cope in some fashion with both the void its passing creates and the forces that contributed to its diminution as an imperative influence in human affairs.

It is accurate to observe that three principal reactions have followed upon the retreating influences of Christianity as both a core metaphysic, a cultural ethos and, of no small importance, a racial myth. Two of these responses are relatively esoteric: (1) the rash of nihilistic subjectivist philosophies and (2) the neo-orthodox attempt of religionists to repair the damage to the Christian edifice by chasing modernism and historicism from the temple. The third reflex is the mass secularization of society, the shifting of the prime social orientation away from Christian mythology to one of an inarticulated eclectic neopragmatism. Doubtless some of this rejection of Judeo-Christian or religionistic emphasis was wholesome for reasons we will discuss momentarily, but the rejection has taken man into a spiritual limbo because he has found himself without a gratifying replacing metaphysic, ethic, or myth. He is especially beset by ethical confusion. In destroying the comforting, if equivocal, fables of his cultural religion, he created the problem of rationally facing the ethical dilemma and constructing a more enduring criterion of value. This was—and is—a mighty undertaking, far more demanding than mass man assumed it to be. He has responded (and here can be included the bulk of contemporary ethical thought) by avoiding the issue and as a result he gambols on the edge of the abyss. Personal spiritual travail and cultural trauma are the fruits.

What caused Christianity to be toppled from its central cultural preeminence? Three factors seem contributive: (1) It abandoned the serious contemplation of metaphysical or theological truth for rather vacuous social prescription. It jettisoned the problem of the soul for the problem of the social being. This proved disastrous, for Christianity's social prescriptions were from the outset both nebulous and fragmentary. At the same time, failing to develop its primary position, Christianity proceeded into the twentieth century with a patched-up, obsolete, and frankly undefendable theology. It certainly was not a theology for the century under the impact of science and analytical philosophy. The end-product was the growing alienation of religion and culture.

(2) Christianity failed to provide a cogent ethical alternative. It compounded its confused ethical pronouncements which, if they had a base at all, were rooted in amalgams of picturesque medieval theories of natural law or neo-Calvinist suspicions of the natural world. In either case, Christian ethics, still encumbered with a hopelessly dualistic concept of human nature, drifted further from a reconciliation with man as a total organism and began to substitute for moral reflection homely platitudes and pious epigrams and replaced hard-minded ethics with criticisms of social mores. It abandoned the natural man for a curious facsimile of its own reassuring making.

(3) Christianity failed utterly, it must be said, to reinterpret candidly and thoughtfully its mythology for the twentieth century mind. It may be generally agreed that religion, whatever else it may be, is a set of archetypal projections. These are clothed in the mantle of symbol, narrated in the language of myth. But archetypal images, while perhaps fundamental in essence, are historically manifested—the mythic mask must change and fit the emerging *zeitgeist*. The nature of myth requires metamorphosis.

Examine the customary Christian Sunday school literature and you will find either smug, patronizing, even pernicious encomiums on the risks of going steady and the like, or rather repelling illustrated versions of the life of Jesus of Nazareth, depicting him as an apparently ineffectual and ascetic Nordic in a vague Levantine costume, feeding a group of sheep of obviously Anglo-Saxon breeding, seemingly in a sort of Rousseau-like reverie, considering what new boons to offer humanity such as treading on bodies of water, raising corpses, changing water into more substantial beverages, or healing lepers at a stroke. Surely, this cannot do as a satisfying mythology for contemporary man.

The twentieth century man's spiritual plight is in part his lack of a functioning mythology, not just as superficial balm, but because myth is a conveyance of truth. In his supposed purging of myth, man created a deep spiritual void, an unanswered yearning. D. H. Lawrence, hardly an admirer of conventional religion, spoke of man's need for "cosmic piety," and this general lack of reverence and awe promulgated by mythological projection has raised in our milieu the social ego to inflated dimension with the attendant frustrations which imperious and unrelenting egos invariably produce—in societies as in individual men.

Traumas heal as do the wounds of the flesh, and we await the revivification of our mythic inheritance.

The Redefinition of Social Freedom

As the social drama of the century unfolds before us, we can observe a curious and disturbing paradox: individualism is declining and yet there is a mood of rebellion against the confinements of social regulation. Put somewhat facetiously, ours is the era of both the ant-hill community, the monotony of social regularity, *and* the topless bathing suit. What is clear is that our social practice is changing faster than our publicly professed convictions. In this connection, our contemporary art and literature are safer guides to the current flux of mind than the remarks of PTA lecturers and commencement speakers.

This much can be said: (1) Economic circumstances have vitiated many of our accustomed social forms (the family may here be cited as illustration), and our urbanized interdependencies have produced a new and more highly routinized and regimented social order. It is in this sense that the individualism of our not too distant past recedes.

(2) This submergence of the individual and the destruction of earlier communal forms—the replacement of *gemeinschaft* by *gesellschaft,* if you wish—has had a twofold result: the unmasking of a number of inhibiting social dogmas, while, at the same time, throttling off certain social outlets and providing the motivation for various types of revolt.

(3) The strong possibility exists that we may be confronted by a society that has grown too free of individual risk, too sanitized, too protective, too colorless, and too apt to express its convictions in self-congratulatory pomposity.

These conclusions suggest a certain measure of social schizophrenia—and this is a legitimate surmise, especially if American culture is the point of focus. We have in fact *two* societies and *two* social ideologies and we lust after each, but cannot really possess both however we strain our sense of honesty and credulity. Neither, one should quickly add, is altogether to be viewed as an optimum climate.

How could these dual orientations be characterized? Without attempting a lengthy analysis, these opposites could be suggested: on the one hand we have the phenomenon of mass demonstration and mass violence, some of which appears to be without evident causation, frequently youthful displays of irritation, truculence, and exuberance with little ideological significance. Link this into the syndrone of *anomie* with what *Time* rather gratuitously termed the "sexual revolution" and add the mounting fascination with the "sick" ideograph—the sick novel, play, art, and joke.

Match this against the equally intense social endorsement of security of an economic and status variety, the whole organizational juggernaut. Add growing evidences of social discomfiture with controversy and a wish for the protective coloration of some uncritical consensus. On this side of the balance place the increasing pressure for censorship, social regulation, restruction of individual choice and behavior on the grounds of some imagined collective welfare.

Or take another form of the paradox: consider our prime merchandising appeal. We are told that the ultimate values of life lie in sexual aggression or, at least, sublimation in some form or other. From hair oils and soft drinks to automobiles, we live in a world of libidinal enticements; we are promised a wondrous paradise of erotic indulgence if only we direct our consumption in the right channels. But, alas, this is clearly a mirage. The promises are not kept, since, on the other hand, the real verities of social attitude do not permit this degree of permissiveness, and we are faced with either making our peace with what is essentially a neo-puritan society or attempting the sly transgressions with their potentialities for risk at the worst and, at the best, the forms of guilt, large and small, that are the by-products of this social heresy.

This is, like all manifestations of schizophrenia, immensely exhausting and brutally expensive in terms of emotional well-being. How long we can afford the waste nurtured by these paradoxical social attitudes is a serious question. It is frankly hopeless to hanker after the simplicities of our forebears, and this realization forces us to reject any sentimental reformulation of past formulae however nostalgically idyllic they may appear. Our contemporary social attitudes must rest on at least three important premises if we are to cure our social schizophrenia and its latent propensities for social conflict.

First, we must desanitize and deregularize our basic patterns of living to the extent that the possibilities for self-definition, self-realization, and self-exploration are revived. Life must continue to be a quest, a risk, with all the variegated experience that infers. We must restore the conception that individual cultivation and individual choice are still crucial factors in the life process and in the determinations of social performance. Safety is never very satisfying in the long run; excitement and the stimulation of uncertainty are vital to the propagation of individual gratification.

Second, we must redefine and vigorously endorse an uncompromising concept of social freedom. It is unquestionably true that one of the causes of our bifurcated social values has been the dispelling of a vast body of restrictive and unwholesome social inhibition as a result of the very considerable broadening of our knowledge of the human personality through the enlightenment of dynamic psychology. We have pulled the veil of ignorance, guilt, and suspicion from much of what comprises human-ness, yet the social correlates of these understandings and freedoms are still to be realized. They must be forthcoming, however alarming they may seem to many whose orientations make such a permissive commitment threatening and disagreeable. If man is to endure much of the diminishment of his prerogatives as a result of socioeconomic circumstances, it is all the more imperative that we protect and enhance the freedom of the individual in his social involvements and extend the permissive flexibility of his social choices. To do less is to court eventual disaster.

Third, social freedom (in any sense of that phrase) brings with it a corresponding ethical demand. Our society hungers for some ethical consistency. Much of our moral confusion and even coarseness arises from a popular misconception as to the nature of the ethical. Consider for a moment what the word "immoral" provokes in the popular mind? Certainly the strongest connotation is that of sexual promiscuity. But even in a wider sense, immorality suggests more a violation of social attitudes regarding custom than it does the negation of any coherent conceptualization of the nature of value. This sensitivity to the more fundamental character of value is notably lacking, and a frequent preoccupation with the morally trivial denigrates the ethical injunction. Moral relativism is a respectable and arguable point of view in ethical thought, but one suspects that much superficial endorsement of moral relativism is a means of converting the language of ethics to subjective predispositions and ideological biases.

But the kind of social freedom demanded by twentieth century existence requires both a more cogent and a more comprehensive popular vision of the ethical. There is an absence of what Gibbon, in his history of the Roman experience, called "civic virtue," and one hopes that the decline of this communal ethical perception and dedication does not herald a decay similar to that which befell Roman society.

Freedom—increased freedom—we must have, but it has its attendant responsibilities; both freedom and responsibility are the prerequisites of reuniting our troubled and schismatic society.

THE ERA OF ANTI-POLITICS

We of the twentieth century are attempting to conduct our political affairs on a foundation of nineteenth century ideas. Both representative democracy and Marxism are pertinent examples. True, we have made considerable effort to modify and adjust these formulae; nonetheless, essentially the identical political conditions that secured power in the last century have heretofore proven successful in the maintenance of political power in our time. Consider the history of our own political parties or, for illustration, compare Disraeli's "tory democracy" and the "New Deal" or Metternich's "concert of Europe" and the Common Market. We still live under concepts of political structure, legal philosophy and equilibriums of power that are inherited from the past century.

There is some evidence that these nineteenth century structures and harmonies will not survive our hundred year cycle. What is the evidence and what might we anticipate to be the ensuing political climate? The evidence can be summarized under these headings: (1) the growth of widespread antipolitical sentiment; (2) a rejection of legalism; and (3) the decline of the influence of the political moderates. These three conditions we are only now beginning to see in sharp perspective, but they are harbingers of attitudes that may shape the political history of the remaining decades of the century.

There is a major contrast between differing views as to the selection of political alternatives and the rejection of politics in total as a useful or necessary technique in attaining human goals. Put another way: political controversy can consist of the conflict of ideologies *or* it can be argument as to whether political solutions to problems are possible or desirable. A survey of the world political scene strongly suggests the growth of this latter, antipolitical viewpoint. There is a mounting sense of cynicism and frustration over the effectiveness of political machinery in realizing the demands of masses of the population, whether or not these demands are legitimate or justifiable. The consequence is a rejection of conventional political remedies in favor of other forms of action and redress. Four rather impressive examples might be cited.

Two can be located in the United States: the so-called Negro Revolt and the appearance of what is dubbed, quite erroneously it may be said, the political extremism of the right. While usually espousing divergent causes, these very substantial interest groups share a common characteristic: both, in the main, distrust and reject the customary political techniques. The procedures of nineteenth century compromise run counter to the mystiques of both movements; the processes of delay and assimilation, both critical aspects of nineteenth century moderation, are thought to be too burdensome in their conception of doctrinaire justice. Moreover, both groups reveal a deep-seated addiction to a conspiratorial view of political function; they are united in the belief that the political process is a tool of insidious and corrupt "establishments" and secret juntas. The end-product is a moralistically couched dismissal of political process from ballot box to legislative action and the substitution of more radical forms of direct action.

Europe provides another illustration. On that continent, the younger age groups have literally fled from the political encounter, vociferously castigating all political ideologies, parties and leaders as hopelessly archaic, venal, stupid, dangerous, and defunct. Their cynicism is startling. There was a time, for instance, when you would well expect a young Englishman to show a lusty enthusiasm for the Labour party as a vehicle for the alteration of the *status quo* he thought he fervently desired. No more; today, the fury is turned upon all political parties and hierarchies indiscriminately. The reasoning of European youth is frequently capricious, oversentimental and self-gratifying, but the attitude is there, deep, articulate, and sweeping.

The behavior of newly created nation-states often reveals a similar disdain for political remedy. Both foreign and domestic policies of a large number of such states shows a convinced antipolitical predilection. This condition has thrown the practice of international relations into a disturbing era in which the accustomed verities of national behavior no longer seem to apply.

In candor, these antipolitical elements subscribe to their view out of an abiding sense of moral rightness. This is both the curious and insurrectionary character of this trend. The belief that moral conviction overrides all other considerations is especially to be noted in the intensifying assault on legalism. Here the proposition is that moral conviction must take precedence over legal right or practice. Law becomes a tired and privilege-plagued anachronism that can and must be swept away before the imperative of moral feeling. The illustrations are legion—from the pronouncements of Martin Luther King to the rationale contrived by the Israeli government for the frankly unorthodox apprehension and trial of Eichmann. The poignant aspect of this antilegalism is that, to use the same examples, many of Dr. King's aspirations are laudable and Eichmann was apparently guilty, at the very least, of complicity with crimes of almost incredible barbarism. Indeed, often within the bastion of legalism itself comes an attack on law as remedy, substituting moral justification. It may be argued that certain recent decisions of the United States Supreme Court are germane samples.

However gaudily this antilegalism may be clothed in moral righteousness, two reservations have to be submitted. First, moral conviction, even if totally sincere, is a quicksilver base for social justice in that it can and frequently is the product of either sentimental emotionalism or radically subjective values. Second, a very persuasive argument can be made for the proposition that the growth of political democracy is substantially a growth of legal guarantees. It is a palpable anxiety that we may exchange the admittedly imperfect institutions of law for the chaos of quarreling claims of moral priority.

It is this matter of imperfection that provokes the attack on legalism. Our age has generated a vulgar passion for total solutions, even simplified total solutions. Realizable or no, the mounting impatience with the somberly attainable is a potentially dangerous trend.

Will the next forty years see the downfall of the moderates from their accustomed seats of power? Some indications suggest this eventuality. They are certainly under vigorous pressure and this harassment will likely continue to gain momentum. Even in the Soviet Union, this comparatively moderate political ascendency is challenged by the full weight of doctrinaire extremism, from within as well as from without. The moderate political coalitions of the West are beginning to creak, to say the least. Moderate politicians in Africa and Asia find their positions increasingly precarious and the flood of circumstances provokes even this minority of statemen into postures of immoderation. The United States has recently observed a political contest in which there were introduced half-obscured motifs not altogether familiar to the credo of political moderation.

The drift is clearly schismatic, with the once formidable moderates caught in the diminishing center. To the ends of the spectrum of political choice gravitate accelerating surges of power, and while it is rash to predict what political forms the future may take, it is not too venturesome to suppose that we are going to endure a period of vigorous political experimentation in which extreme alternatives, previously viewed as unacceptably radical, may be tried. What will be the ultimate conclusion of this wider swing of the political pendulum must be answered by what Hegel referred to as the "inevitable verdict of history." Let us hope it is not more violent than we can absorb.

We are constantly reminded, usually in turgidly pompous prose that we live in a century of crisis, a century of decision, a century of ultimate choice. The grim alternatives are endlessly depicted; the human imagination was undoubtedly provided with a sharp stimulus by the cataclysm of Hiroshima and subsequent demonstrations of man's destructive hardware. The great bulk of these gloomy forebodings divide into two answers to a single question.

The question is: How will the world end? And the answers are that we will blow ourselves up, either accidently or with malice aforethought, or that, alternatively, we will suffocate from spiritual deprivation—the "not with a bang but a whimper" school of thought.

The question has a certain undeniable legitimacy. Will we witness Armaggeddon in the twentieth century? It appears we have the implements to put on this sort of a spectacle. Or, will we retreat, without the actual holocaust, into the darkness of a new barbarism, fretting over the malfunctionings of our power-driven toothbrushes while the Oriental hordes beat on the gates? Or, will we gradually enslave ourselves to the guidance of a cunning elite corps of psychiatric manipulators and recreational consultants?

No prudent man would wish to volunteer a categorical answer as to whether the "big bang" will or will not be the exclamation point terminating the century. Who can predict the caprices of human irrationality?

But to the query regarding the possibility of our gradually slipping into the twilight of our civilization (at least as we have known it since Socrates sipped his last libation), there may be a more definite response. The answer must be *yes*. There exists the historical possibility that our civilization could succumb and be replaced by a form of life representing wholesale negation of those values that have provided the core definitions of Western civilization. And this need not necessarily be the result of either nuclear derangements and military inundations from the Eurasian Steppe. It could be the result of a cultural paralysis conceivably born of mass fear and mass deadening of the faculty of criticism and judgment.

Modern man is very evidently afraid, and he does not really know what he is afraid of and this intensifies his anxiety. He often tries to label it by saying that he is afraid of The Bomb, but he really isn't. It is something else. And the fear spreads, casting patterns of restless and aimless anxiety, draining strength and efficiency from our social institutions and maiming our creative potential. Even the most cursory glimpse of the past two decades reveals the impact of the fear—our society grows humorless, hostile, trivial, compulsive, and generally morose.

Conversely, our society seems bent on a frenzied pursuit of consumption and amusement. By themselves, material comfort, amusement and indulgence are worthy of sensible cultivation, but not as dreary substitution mechanisms, means of anesthetizing our capabilities and responsibilities for discrimination. The danger is the prospect of a once-proud civilization surrendering its prime freedom, the freedom to choose, to judge critically, to reject, in a vain hope that it can temporarily allay the nagging fear by feeding the grosser appetite.

What could this fear be? Modern man is afraid because he begins to feel that he as an individual no longer has any substantial control over his own destiny. This thought, however he represses it, is appalling, terrifying. He has, he thinks, become merely an instrument, indeed a part of a gigantic machine he does not and perhaps could not understand. He fears he cannot alter his life's course by the exercise of his own will.

Of course, at no stage of history has man ever been fully the master of his separate fate, but it is also unavoidably true that in the twentieth century the scope of individual decision and action, as it affects the life process, has been drastically reduced, or at least so it appears. The addition of the qualifying "so it appears" points to the fact that contemporary man's fear that he has lost his power over himself may be partially irrational. No reflective man has ever shown much enthusiasm for the personalistic arrogance of the sentiments expressed in Henley's *Invictus*. Modern man has been, in one sense, *over*individualized since the Enlightenment; he must now understand and learn to revere rather than be suspicious of his ontic interrelatedness and perceive that these primordial connections are not to be confused with the sterile interdependencies of the industrial society against which he covertly rebels. He must know and accept what it is to be a social creature in the most fundamental sense of that term.

As well, he must realize that he yet does exercise decisive and significant personal power and that individual will must be basically defined as judgment. He has erred in confusing the areas of action and judgment and therefore has mistakenly assumed that the curtailment of action is tantamount to a crippling reduction of personal influence. The closing of a physical frontier has little to do with the range and importance of judgment, except perhaps to make the latter all the more imperative.

Twentieth century man need not destroy himself and his civilization out of fear of existential emasculation since such an operation must be self-performed.